IRISH WAKE AMUSEMENTS

Irish Wake Amusements

SEÁN Ó SÚILLEABHÁIN

MERCIER PRESS

MERCIER PRESS
PO Box 5, 5 French Church Street, Cork
and
16 Hume Street, Dublin

*Trade enquiries to CMD Distribution, 55a Spruce Avenue,
Stillorgan Industrial Park, Blackrock, Dublin*

Translated by the author from the original Irish *Caitheamh
Aimsire ar Thórraimh* by An Clóchomhar in 1961.
© This translation, Mercier Press, 1967
This edition 1997

A CIP is available for this book from the British Library

ISBN 1 85635 173 4

10 9 8 7 6 5 4 3 2 1

Printed in Ireland by Colour Books Ltd.

CONTENTS

INTRODUCTION

During the spring of 1921, I happened to be a student attending a Preparatory School some miles from Ballina, in Co. Mayo. It was a very disturbed period of Ireland's history. Ambushes, shootings and burnings were of daily occurrence in many areas, and Mayo too had its share of these. Still, despite everything, the traditional rural life went on as it had done for centuries.

A death occurred in the district at that time, and I accompanied some of my fellow-students to the wake at night. The house was a long, thatched one, with a fairly large kitchen. The corpse was laid out on the 'hag-bed', beside the fireplace. The kitchen was crowded when we entered; some were seated on stools and chairs along the walls, while others sat on their knees. As we knew the people of the house, we shook their hands and sympathised with them in their sorrow. We then knelt down on the clay floor beside the bed and offered a silent prayer for the soul of the deceased. Room was made for for us in a corner of the kitchen, and a clay pipe, filled with tobacco, was handed to each of us. We accepted the pipes, although none of us was at the stage of using them, and said the customary prayer: May God have mercy on the souls of the dead! We attempted to 'redden' the pipes, out of respect for the deceased, but only in a half-hearted way.

Within a short time, the house became more crowded than ever. More people were arriving than leaving. As far as I can now recall, no other room except the kitchen was in use for the occasion. Tobacco smoke pervaded the whole place, and everybody was perspiring, as the night was close and heavy. Conversation went on in both Irish and English, and current topics were discussed in the manner usual on such occasions.

At this point, there entered a local man who was well known to all present. He was a rather simple fellow, poor and harmless, and had never worn shoes. He was the butt of many jokes on the part of some of the locals; still, they all had a concealed liking for him. On this occasion, he was barefoot, as usual, and his hair was long and shaggy. He knelt down beside the corpse and recited an Our Father and Hail Mary aloud, his arms extended towards the bed. The kitchen fell silent as the people listened to him pray. As he was about to get to his feet, the prayer over, a fellow, who was near me in the corner, called to him:

'Say them again, John!'

The simple fellow went down on his knees again and repeated the same prayers aloud. By this time, titters of laughter were breaking out among the crowd.

'I wouldn't doubt you, John!' called another fellow. 'Say them again!'

While poor John was reciting the prayers aloud for the third time, laughter and amusement had spread through the kitchen. Over a period of ten minutes, he said the prayers six or seven times, until he was finally allowed to rise to his feet and make his way to a seat in a corner.

The wake had become much more lively by this time. There was a good deal of laughter. Young lads started to push and crush one another on the stools. A few of them chanced to be seated on a sack of potatoes at the bottom of the kitchen, and a large potato was thrown at a man who had bent down to converse with somebody. He wheeled around but couldn't detect the culprit. The potato-throwing then became general; all and sundry were the targets, so long as the pelting could be done without detection. The only light in the kitchen came from a single lamp and from the candles beside the corpse, so that those who were intent on mischief had semi-darkness in their favour.

Nor were potatoes the only missiles. Water from a bucket near the dresser was splashed on people who had their backs turned; and young fellows who had no use for the clay pipes broke off the shanks and aimed them here and there. Horse-play became the order of the night.

I had never experienced a wake like this in my home county, Kerry, and what surprised me most of all was that the people of the house, who were mourning the loss of a relative, made no attempt to curb the unruly behaviour. The women of the house, an old lady and her daughter-in-law, remained seated near the fire, chatting with neighbours and relatives, while the man of the house made his way here and there through the kitchen, welcoming new arrivals and bidding farewell to those who were leaving. None of them seemed to be resentful of the misbehaviour, nor did they appear to take any notice of it.

My companions and myself left the wake-house after a few hours and returned to our lodgings. Next day, we were told that we had missed a great night of fun and games, which were played after we had left.

The memory of that wake-night in Mayo has remained impressed on my mind ever since, so different was it from what I was used to in my home district of South Kerry. Yet whenever, through later years, I mentioned my experience to others, I learned that lively, merry wakes had been the normal type throughout most of Ireland. They were on the wane, however, and would soon be only a memory.

I decided, therefore, to try to collect accounts of old-time Irish wakes from sources such as books, journals and newspapers. I examined all the published reports I could find of the Synodal Decrees of bishops, with special reference to the Statutes dealing with wakes, both for Ireland and other countries, down through the centuries. I have translated from the original Latin the relevant passages. To supplement what was available in print, I questioned many persons from different parts of the country who had knowledge and, in most cases, personal experience of wakes in olden times. While the results of my research are not as complete as I would wish,

11

still I hope that the reader will get a picture of traditional practices which, though current for centuries, are almost unknown to the present generation.

In the final chapter, I have attempted to explain how the wake itself may have originated, and the reasons why these, now solemn, occasions were formerly gay and hilarious. It will be seen that our ancestors were but continuing a centuries-old custom, which prevailed not only in Ireland but in other parts of the world also, a custom whose origin and significance had become obscured with the passage of time.

SEÁN Ó SÚILLEABHÁIN

I

WAKES AT PRESENT AND LONG AGO[1]

The waking of the dead is a very ancient custom throughout the world. Extant accounts of wakes in Europe go back almost a thousand years. The practice has died out, however, on most of the continent of Europe within the past century[2].

It still survives in Ireland and is likely to continue so for some time. The passage of time brings many changes however, and wakes too have been affected to a greater or lesser degree in the past hundred years, or so. Old people who have had experience of both former wakes and present-day ones give witness to the great changes which have taken place. Nowadays, the wake is a solemn occasion in most areas, even when the deceased is 'no great loss,' as the saying goes. And the purpose of a visit to a wake is to pray for the dead and to sympathise with the relatives of the dead person.

Let us first take a look at the main features of wakes as they are today, before describing what they were like in earlier times. Interesting though the innumerable customs and beliefs be which are brought into play at a time of death, an account of most of them would be out of place in this book, which seeks only to describe the wake and its attendant practices today and formerly.

When somebody dies in rural Ireland nowadays, the body is waked in the house until it is taken to the church on the evening before the day of burial. As soon as it is evident that death has supervened, preparations are made to lay out the corpse for the wake. The laying out is usually done by a few neighbouring women, who have had practice in doing so on other occasions; they wash the body, put on the habit and get ready the bed on

13

which the corpse will be laid. In the case of a man, who has been accustomed to shave himself, the shaving of the corpse is carried out by a neighbour before the habit is put on. A crucifix is placed on the breast and rosary beads are entwined in the fingers, sheets are hung over the bed and along two or three of the sides, and candles are lighted in candlesticks near the remains. These tasks take about two hours to complete. Details of the custom vary, of course, from one area to another, but the main observance is much the same everywhere.

The relatives do not cry or keen the dead, as a rule, until the body has been laid out. The women, having finished their task, now withdraw from the bedside, and their place is taken by the immediate relatives, who express their grief in either muffled sobs or loud wailing, according to the depth of their sorrow. The keening is most intense and heartfelt where the deceased is considered a 'great loss' – a parent, who has left a large, young family behind, or somebody who has died at an early age or tragically. After a while, the mourners are quietly approached by a few of the neighbours, consoled, and led away from the bedside.

If death occurs in the evening or at night, and if the news of it does not spread, by means of a shop or village nearby, only the close neighbours will have heard about it, and they and the relatives will be the main mourners at the wake that night. News is sent to distant relatives, however, as soon as possible.

At dawn next morning, two men set out to bring the requirements for the wake from the nearest town. These are usually one of the relatives and a neighbour. They order the coffin (which, in olden times, was made by a local carpenter at the wake-house) and return in the evening with whatever is necessary: bread, meat and so on to provide meals, as well as whiskey and stout, wine, pipes, tobacco and snuff. A meal and a drink or more are given to all visitors, and a clay pipe, filled with tobacco, if such are available, or else pipefuls of tobacco, are offered to all. A plateful of snuff is taken about the kitchen. Those who take a pinch of it or who accept a pipe bless themselves, saying: The blessing of God on the souls of the dead.

The place where the corpse is laid out is usually decided on by the relatives, according to the convenience afforded by the house. It may be a table, a settle or bed in the kitchen or in one of the rooms, or else, if there is a suitable loft, upstairs. Traditional custom demands that the corpse must not be left unattended for the duration of the wake; one or more persons, usually women, sit nearby[3]. On entering a wake-house, a person makes his way to the side of the corpse, wherever it be, kneels down and silently recites a few prayers for the departed soul. He is then welcomed by one or more of the relatives and expresses his sympathy: 'I'm sorry for your trouble', or some similar words. He speaks kindly of the deceased and then moves away, if he finds that the people of the house have many visitors to welcome and attend to. He is offered a drink and food during the hours he spends at the wake, either inside the kitchen, if the weather is inclement, or outside, where most of the men congregate, if the weather is fine.

The wake-house is visited during the day mainly by old men and old women, who arrive and leave as it suits them. Most remain for at least a few hours, during which hospitality is shown to them. At nightfall, when the day's work is over, the neighbours, and parishioners generally, make their way to the wake-house and remain there until about midnight. All are shown the same hospitality.

The Rosary is recited once or twice during the night, around midnight, and again towards morning[4]. That has been the traditional custom in Ireland for centuries, so far as can be ascertained. A schoolmaster or someone who is locally acknowledged as a leader on social occasions starts the prayer and recites the first decade, followed by the relatives of the deceased, if they suffice in numbers. In olden times, there was a special Rosary for the dead, followed by many other prayers which have now gone out of popular use. The Rosary is said around the corpse, while all who are anywhere in the house kneel and recite the responses.

Most of the visitors to a wake go home about midnight in twos or threes, on foot if they have no other means of conveyance. Only the relatives and close neighbours remain until morning. They pass the time in conversation about local and national affairs, and tea or some stronger beverage is partaken of. Even humorous anecdotes are told and a titter of laughter may be heard, but, in general, the atmosphere is solemn and decorous.

If the person dies late in the evening or at night, the main wake is not held until the following night, when a much larger crowd is present. The second night is intended to give neighbours who had not been present on the previous night, as well as distant relatives, an opportunity of attending. The corpse is now generally brought to the local church on the evening prior to the burial. There are thus two funerals: one on that evening, and the second to the graveyard next day. When the corpse has been delivered at the church, only the relatives, accompanied by a few neighbours, return to the house of mourning. Once the interment has taken place, the people of the house spend a few days restoring the house to its normal condition, with the help of the neighbours. Life then resumes its former rhythm.

Food and Drink at Wakes

In the old days, as now, food and drink were a necessary feature of wakes[5]. The difference is that much more alcohol was consumed formerly than is the case at present. Beer or stout were a rarity in Ireland in olden times, or even unknown in many places, so that whiskey and poteen were the main potent drinks. Whether it was that these drinks were too strong or that most men were unused to them, except on rare occasions, it is clear from the accounts in printed sources and from oral evidence that drunkenness was more common then than it is now. To make matters worse, most houses were small, and when a wake occurred, were overcrowded and badly ventilated. Thus, the heavy atmosphere combined with the alcohol and, occasionally, the smoke to cause drunkenness at wakes. Unruly behaviour and the playing of games on such occasions often reached unseemly proportions.

Many references to the drinking of alcohol at wakes and funerals are to be met with in books: (a) Sir Henry Bourgchier described in 1623 how hundreds of horsemen, with twice that number of men on foot, attended funerals and joined in the feasting which would impoverish the relatives of the dead person for ever more[6]; (b) J. G. Prim wrote about a law passed by the Corporation of Kilkenny on June 25, 1638, which forbade the mayor to partake of food or drink at a wake; penalty for disobedience, £10[7]; (c) John Dunton, an English traveller, wrote a number of letters in the middle of the 17th century which described, among other things, the feasting and drinking which he had witnessed in Ireland on the morning of a funeral[8]; (d) Sir Henry Piers, with reference to Co. Westmeath in 1682, told of the beer drunk and the tobacco smoked at wakes[9]; (e) Edward MacLysaght quotes a description of a wake in Co. Kildare in 1683[10]: 'Their wakes also over dead corpses, where they have a table spread and served with the best that can be had at such a time, and after a while attending (in expectation the departed soul will partake) they fall to eating and drinking, after to revelling, as if one of the feasts of Backus' (sic); (f) Thomas Campbell described in 1778 the wakes which he saw in Ireland as occasions for merriment and feasting, where people assembled from far and near; the grown-ups among them passed the time in smoking and drinking whiskey – so much, Campbell thought, that the relatives of the deceased would be impoverished for evermore. He told of a poor woman who had laid by a few guineas to cover her own burial expenses, and who started to beg in order that those few guineas might remain intact to supply the neighbours with plenty of whiskey and tobacco at her wake and funeral[11]; (g) Maria Edgeworth in 1810 described the wakes of her time[12]: pipes and tobacco were first distributed and, if money were available, cakes, beer and whiskey were also given out. She concluded her account with the following verse:

Deal on, deal on, my merry men all,
Deal on your cakes and your wine;
For whatever is dealt at her funeral today
Shall be dealt to-morrow at mine;

(h) Rev. Horatio Townsend, describing wakes in Co. Cork at the same period, wrote[13]: 'The room, where the body is laid out dressed in white, is filled with people, regaling themselves with liquor and tobacco, and chatting on various topics, one of which is praise of the deceased'; (i) T. Crofton Croker, in 1824, wrote[14]: 'The wake of a corpse is a scene of merriment rather than of mourning. The body lies exposed in the coffin for two or three nights previous to interment, surrounded by many candles, and with the face uncovered. To avert misfortune arising from the death of the heads of families, when a man dies his head is placed at the foot of the bed; but this ceremony is not deemed necessary with women, and they are allowed to remain in the usual position. In the evening a general assembly of the neighbours takes place, when they are entertained with whiskey, tobacco and snuff'; (j) J. N. Brewer, a year later, wrote that the supply of pipes, tobacco, snuff, whiskey and other delicacies was limited only by the financial resources of the family, who were happy at having a large wake, with feasting and drinking, to lessen their own sorrow[15]; (k) Mrs. S. C. Hall[16] disliked the wakes she saw in 1841; disreputable things occurred, she said, as there was no shortage of whiskey, and both men and women drank to excess[17].

In addition to the foregoing accounts, old people of our own day, who attended wakes in their younger days, bear testimony to the amount of drinking and, sometimes, of drunkenness, which occurred. It is not to be wondered at, therefore, that the attention of both the bishops and the clergy in general came to be directed on such wakes, and every effort was made to curb the abuses. Here follow some directives issued by episcopal Synods and by individual bishops towards this end.

Archdiocese of Armagh

The Synod of bishops, on three occasions (1660, 1668 and 1670)[18] ordered that drinking at wakes should be abolished. On the third occasion, they forbade the distribution in wake-houses of whiskey or brandy; if this rule were disobeyed, they said, no priest would have any connection with either the wake or the funeral. Any priest who was negligent in stopping this practice would be deprived of his parish. The abuse seems to have continued, however, for, on October 8, 1860 (almost two hundred years later), the Synod of bishops again forbade the drinking of alcohol at funerals.

The Synod of Tuam (1660)

Statute 20 of this Synod ordered people to give up excessive drinking and feasting at Catholic wakes; and it suggested that the wrongdoers be advised to give most, if not all, of the money spent in that way, to the poor as alms, or else to spend it on Masses for the souls of the dead[19].

The Synod of Clones (23/8/1670)

This Synod ordered that an end be put to drinking at wakes, and went on to forbid the holding of wakes at all for the future[20].

The Diocese of Waterford and Lismore

The clergy of the diocese met at Carrick-on-Suir in the year 1676, Most Rev. Dr. John Brenan presiding. It was ordered that drinking at wakes should cease, because of the loss of souls caused by it, as well as the insult given to God[21].

The Diocese of Kilmore

Drinking at wakes was forbidden in 1687[22]. In the year 1750, the bishop of the diocese, Dr. Laurence Richardson, in an account of the state of religion within his domain[23], which he sent to Rome, stated that the orders and the earnestness of a predecessor of his, Michael MacDonagh, O.P., seemed to have had the effect of terminating, during the previous two years, the sinful practice of providing alcoholic liquors at funerals, as if they were festive occasions. He further mentioned that this custom had been widely prevalent in certain parts of the diocese previously, causing unchristian behaviour, drunkenness, poverty and, too often, death itself.

The Archdiocese of Cashel and Emly

In the course of a pastoral letter concerning abuses at wakes and funerals issued about the year 1800 to the clergy and laity of the dioceses of Cashel and Emly, the bishop, Most Rev. Dr. Thomas Bray, said[24]: 'We likewise most strictly forbid all persons to distribute, or give out at wakes of funerals whiskey, or spirits, or strong liquors of any sort, in ever so small a quantity, to any person, through any consideration or pretext whatever. And all heads of families, whoever they be, men or women, who order or suffer whiskey, or strong liquors of any sort, to be distributed at wakes or funerals, are, in like manner, to be reprimanded in the chapel, and deprived of Sacraments, until they have made a public submission before the altar, for their criminal disobedience to the order of the Church, with a solemn promise never again to be guilty of the same transgression. And we most earnestly exhort all pious, devout persons, who may be at wakes or funerals, where such odious, pernicious, and detestable practices take place, to give immediate notice thereof to the Parish Priest. Moreover, we strictly charge all our clergy, secular and regular, not to celebrate Mass at the wakehouse, nor bless the clay, nor accompany the funeral to the place of burial, where they discover that whiskey, or spirits of any sort, are given out.'

The bishop also gave orders that 'the foregoing instructions and regulations, respecting wakes and funerals, are to be read once in Advent every year until they are no longer necessary; and should also be repeated as often as occasion may require, and where necessary, should also be explained in Irish'.

The Archdiocese of Dublin

In the Statutes issued by this Synod in July, 1831, priests were ordered to forbid their congregations to provide tobacco at wakes or to spend money on things which would lead people to commit sin. The bishops disparaged and condemned the custom of providing alcoholic drinks at funerals, stating that such would cause great harm to a christian people. They gave orders to the clergy to make this Statute known to their flocks frequently; and, if they deemed it necessary, they were to warn the people that they would bless neither the corpse nor the grave unless this abominable practice ceased.[25]

The Parish of Tydavnet, Co. Monaghan

A regulation which was in force there in 1832 stated that, if anybody died in the parish, no priest would attend the funeral unless some responsible person promised that no pipes or tobacco would be given out for smoking in the graveyard or on the way to it on the funeral day[26].

The Diocese of Ardagh

In October, 1835, the clergy of the diocese met under the chairmanship of Most Rev. Dr. William Higgins. Among the statements issued was one to the effect that the custom of giving out alcoholic drinks at funerals, which was on the decline in certain areas should be generally discontinued; and parish priests were ordered to so inform their congregations[27].

Synod of Irish Bishops

A meeting of bishops in Maynooth in 1875 completely forbade the practice, which was a disgrace to christian communities, of giving out alcoholic drinks at wakes or near graveyards. Bishops were urged to penalise those who were found guilty of such misbehaviour[28].

Archdiocese of Dublin
John Coulter states in *Curious Notions*[29] that Most Rev. Dr. Walsh issued a pastoral letter, which was to be read in all Catholic churches in the Archdiocese on March 23, 1890, condemning the practice of drinking at wakes, funerals, and on other occasions.

Diocese of Ferns
Included among the Statutes published for this diocese in 1898 was one which urged the clergy to put an end to the popular custom of wasting money on wake-goods, which could lead people into sin[30].

Diocese of Ardagh and Clonmacnoise
His Lordship, Most. Rev. Dr. Hoare, issued a notice, which was to be displayed in all churches in the diocese on February 17, 1903, forbidding the drinking of alcohol at wakes or funerals under the pain of mortal sin. Mass would not be offered in any house in which the regulation was broken.

The task of enforcing regulations like these fell upon the shoulders of the parish priests and curates in individual parishes. This was probably done by means of sermons and on other suitable occasions, such as at parish 'stations', in the confessional, and at wakes and funerals as well. It is evident that the condemned practices had a tenacious hold on the people, since bishops in individual dioceses had to repeat their condemnation time after time. It is possible that many other decrees were issued in Ireland condemning drinking at wakes and funerals, but it is difficult or impossible to consult them now.

It must be pointed out that Ireland had hundreds of distilleries a few centuries ago. Whiskey was the usual drink on social occasions – at fairs and markets, at patterns, at weddings, at wakes and funerals. Poteen was in large supply too in many areas. It is not to be wondered at, therefore, that the bishops and clergy took whatever steps they could to end abuses. Viewed from present-day conditions, it can be said that clerical opposition to harmful practices associated with wakes and funerals did finally have its effect. Wakes today are comparatively sober affairs.

Ireland was not the only country in which feasting, heavy drinking, and the use of tobacco and snuff were important features of wakes and funerals. They were all part of a widespread common pattern of popular custom throughout Europe, in Iceland and elsewhere. Any excesses which drew the reprobation of the Irish clergy were in keeping with similar practices in other countries. We have references in printed sources to these for England[31], Scotland[32], Wales[33], the Isle of Man[34], Sweden[35], Norway[36], France[37], Germany[38], the Balkan lands[39] and the United States of America[40].

The cost of providing the means for such celebrations at wakes and funerals must have fallen heavily on the relatives of the deceased. Indeed, many contemporary commentators (mainly foreigners) on this aspect of death customs stated that many families became impoverished on account of it[41].

Feasting and drinking at wakes and funerals had deep roots in European social life. As witness of the opposition of church leaders to abuses in this regard, there has survived a Synodal Statute regarding them, which was issued on the continent as early as the year 306, followed by others in the succeeding centuries[42].

NOTES

1. For a good account of wakes, see Hartmann, *Der Totenkult in Irland*, 151–172.
2. *Handwörterbuch des deutschen Aberglaubens*, V, 1023–1167; Puckle, *Funeral Customs*, 61–.

3. Christiansen, *The Dead and the Living*, 30; Mrs. S. C. Hall, *Ireland*, I, 226, 235.

4. Little, *Malachi Horan Remembers*, 71; *An Claidheamh Soluis*, 3/7/1909, 5.

5. Hartmann, *Totenkult*, 113, 162.

6. *Advertisements for Ireland*, 1623 (edited by George O'Brien), 44.

7. *Jour. Kilk. Arch. Society*, II, 333.

8. MacLysaght, *Irish Life in the Seventeenth Century*, 359–360.

9. *Westmeath* (1682), 124–, 126.

10. *op. cit.*, 321.

11. *A Philosophical Survey of the South of Ireland* (1778), 210–211.

12. *Castle Rackrent* (1810), 214.

13. *Statistical Survey of Cork* (1810), 90.

14. *Researches* (1824), 170–171.

15. *The Beauties of Ireland* (1825), I, clxxxv–vi.

16. *Ireland*, I, 221, 224, 231.

17. See also the following: Brand, *Pop. Antiq.*, II, 147–152; Shaw Mason, *Parochial Survey*, I, 595–6; *ib.*, II, 365, 460; Carleton, *Traits and Stories*, I, 104–5; Little, *Malachi Horan*, 71; Wood-Martin, *Elder Faiths*, 1, 301; Lady Wilde, *Anct. Legends*, 121; Mrs. Houston, *Twenty Years in the Wild West*, 121; Carr, *A Stranger in Ireland*, 257–8; Mac-Donagh, *Irish Life and Character*, 374; Blake, *Letters from the Irish Highlands*, 335; Coulter, *Curious Notions*, 58; *Ethnography of the Mullet, etc.* (Proc. R. I. Academy, 3rd. series, III, No. 4), 622; Ó Ruadháin, *Pádhraic Mháire Bhán*, 118; *Ar Aghaidh*, 12/1936, 5; *Seanchas Ardmhacha*, I, No. 1, 124; *Ireland's Own*, XLVII, 77.

18. *Spicilegium Ossoriense*, II, 199–200; Renehan, *Collections*, 158.

19. Renehan, *op. cit.*, 503.

20. Moran, *Memoirs of Most Rev. Dr. Plunkett*, 127.

21. *Spic. Ossor.*, II, 239–240.

22. O'Connell, *The Diocese of Kilmore*, 496.

23. *Archivium Hibernicum*, V, 132–134.

24. *Statuta Synodalia pro unit. dioec. Cassel et Imelac*, 105–8.

25. *Statuta Dioecesana* (1831), 183–4.

26. *Archivium Hibernicum*, XII, 69.

27. *Statuta Dioecesana* (1834), 98–99.

28. *Acta et Decreta Syn. Plen. Episcop. Hib.* (1877), 146.

29. Coulter, *Curious Notions*, 58, 233–4.

30. *Statuta Dioec. Fernensis* (1898), 61–62.

31. Brand, *Pop. Antiq.*, II, 147–152; Burne, *Shropshire Folklore*, 304–6, 309; Bottrell, *Traditions of West Cornwall*, 83.

32. MacPherson, *Primitive Beliefs*, 125; Dean Ramsay, *Reminiscences*, 54–55, 181–2; Murray, *Scottish Women*, 117, 119; Colin MacDonald, *Echoes of the Glen*, 65; Carment, *Glimpses of the Olden Time*, 38; Simpson, *Folklore in Lowland Scotland*, 201; Mrs. Skith, *Memoirs of a Highland Lady*, 192; Mackintosh, *Notes on Strathdearn*, 34; Stewart, *A Highland Parish*, 158; Alex. MacDonald, *Story and Song*, 155, 161; Guthrie, *Old Scottish Customs*, 99–100, 125–6; *Scottish Notes and Queries*: 3/1890, 156; *ib.* 4/1890, 173; *ib.* 10/1891, 76.

33. Brand, *Pop. Antiq.*, II, 211, 324; *Montgomeryshire Collections*, LII, part 1, 59.

34. Owen, *Welsh Folk Custom*, 173; Waldron, *Description of the Isle of Man*, 170.

35. Hagberg, *När Döden Gäster*, 422–457; Brand, *Pop. Antiq.*, II, 143.

36. Christiansen, *The Dead and the Living*, 29, 32, 37.

37. de Nore, *Coutumes et Mythes et Traditions des Provinces de France* (passim).

38. Christiansen, *op. cit.*, 45.

39. Durham, *Some Tribal Origins, Laws and Customs of the Balkans*, 217–228.

40. Earle, *Customs and Fashions in Old New England*, 364; G. L. Gomme, *English Traditions and Foreign Customs*, 319.

41. Campbell, *Philosophical Survey*, 210–211; Shaw Mason, *Parochial Survey*, II, 365, 460; Bourgchier, *Advertisements for Ireland* (1623), 44; Murray, *Scottish Women*, 119; Stewart, *A Highland Parish*, 158; G. L. Gomme, *English Traditions and Foreign Customs*, 245.

42. Bingham, *Origines Ecclesiasticae*, II, 1251; Migne, *Patrologia latina*, XXXII, 132.

II

STORYTELLING; SINGING; MUSIC AND DANCING; CARD-PLAYING; RIDDLES; TONGUE-TWISTERS AND RHYMING

As has already been said, wakes in Ireland and in other countries in former decades were far from being the solemn occasions which they now are[1]. They were gay, social functions, with merriment and games, except when the deceased was a young person or was regarded as a 'great loss'. They were far merrier than weddings. The young people of every district looked forward with keen anticipation to the death of an old man or woman, which would offer them a 'night of turf-throwing and frivolity'. This type of behaviour was not intended to show disrespect for the dead or for the clergy; rather was it a deeply-rooted traditional custom, which people were loth to discontinue, offering, as it did, some enjoyment and pleasure.

A friend of mine has told me that he saw games being played at the wake of an old man in Conamara in 1959. Although statistics are not available, it is probable that scattered occurrences like this are but rare survivals of what was until the end of the last century the normal pattern. The old-time wakes are now almost things of the past. It is fitting, therefore, to attempt to describe them, before knowledge of them has also vanished. Our forefathers in most parts of the country would have regarded what is described in this book as traditional and normal and correct, from their viewpoint. Let us see what happened at old-time wakes in Ireland and elsewhere.

Storytelling

The start of the night at a wake was usually spent in the kitchen, if there was room for all. Affairs of the day were discussed: local gossip went on, and any big news in the world of politics or such was the subject for comment[2]. In addition, humorous anecdotes were told about local people and happenings, causing a titter of laughter among various groups. Patrick Kennedy, describing wakes in Co. Wexford in his own day (around the middle of the last century)[3], said that the history of the district was a subject for discussion[4].

Most of the visitors to a wake went home about midnight, leaving behind only a dozen or a score of people. After the Rosary had been recited, storytelling began. This was usual even in districts where the more lively type of wake was unknown. My father, who died at the age of 87 sixteen years ago, told me that he had heard many fine, traditional folk-tales at wakes in his native parish of Tuosist, in South Kerry, as a young man[5]. Listening to good storytellers was one of the main amusements in that district at wakes, where other forms of entertainment were absent. The storytelling was carried on everywhere in Ireland, and followed an informal pattern; in one corner of the kitchen, a storyteller, usually an elderly man, sat surrounded by a group of interested listeners, while another recited his tale to a different group elsewhere. It was not difficult to get some good narrators of tales in most districts in former times, especially when the Irish language was the normal means of expression. They were welcomed at wakes, as the stories helped to while away the long night hours and kept the listeners from becoming drowsy or falling asleep towards dawn.

So far as I have been able to discover, the Irish bishops had no fault to find with storytelling at wakes. There was just one exception: Dr. John Brenan, Bishop of Waterford and Lismore, in 1676 described the tales as *ineptae fabulae* (silly stories), and suggested that prayers be recited at wakes instead[6].

Tales are still occasionally told at wakes in the Gaeltacht, but the custom has died out over the greater part of Ireland[7].

Singing

'Sing a song at a wake, and shed a tear when a child is born' – so goes an old Irish saying.

The voice of a good singer gave more pleasure at Irish wakes than any other form of entertainment. Singing on such occasions was widespread here and abroad. Almost a thousand years ago, Burchardt, the German cleric of Worms, castigated such songs, calling them *diabolica carmina* (songs of the Devil)[8]. Irish bishops, too, often condemned the custom[9].

Sir Henry Piers, in his description of Westmeath in 1682, referred to lewd songs being sung at wakes there[10]. *Anthologia Hibernica,* dated December, 1794[11], mentioned singing as part of a wake-game, called *Mac Soipín,* or The Knight of Straw. Describing his journey through East Galway in 1813, Rev. J. Hall mentioned singing at wakes there[12]; so also did T. Crofton Croker in Munster eleven years later[13]. Julius Rodenberg heard merry songs at an Irish wake in 1861[14]; and Patrick Kennedy, in *Banks of the Boro*[15], lists the types of songs which were usually to be heard at wakes in Co. Wexford at the time of the Fenians. William Carleton too gave accounts of the custom[16]; and Henry Morris heard his uncle describe the singing at wakes around Carrickmacross in his younger days[17]. Nor need we depend on written sources for evidence. There are still amongst us many elderly people who heard singing at wakes, or even sang there themselves. But the custom has now died out almost everywhere.

Not every wake had singing as part of the festivities. As already stated, if the deceased was young or deeply regretted, neither singing nor games took place.

The singing was occasionally part of some wake-games. If a forfeit or penalty was to be exacted on somebody as the result of a game, he or she might be called upon to either sing or get a substitute to do so; a further penalty was exacted for non-performance of the original forfeit, involving the burning of a hat or some other garment.

Songs were often sung at wakes for other reasons also. A friend might sing to fulfil a promise to do so given to the deceased, while he still lived. The better the singer, the more enjoyment he gave. I have got accounts even of the relatives of the deceased asking a well-known singer to perform, and of their displeasure, if he refused. An extra drink was given to a good singer in order to humour him to contribute further. Occasionally, groups in different parts of the wake-house vied with each other in producing the best singers and songs, which alternated as the night wore on.

So far as I have been able to discover, lively songs were not frowned upon at wakes. Still, the majority were love songs or patriotic ones, religious songs, or else those which told of sad occurrences. In Conamara, the usual songs were *Baile Uí Lí* (Ballylee), *An Muilleoir Bán* (The White Miller), *Bhí Triúr Mac Agam* (I Had Three Sons) and *Oileán Éide* (Éide Island). Kennedy lists for Wexford *Buachaill na Gruaige Doinne* (The Brownhaired Boy), *An Cailín Rua* (The Redhaired Girl), *Síle Ní Ghadhra*, The Cottage Maid, The Streams of Bunclody and Don't Marry. Thus it would seem that both local songs and those more widely known were popular at wakes[18].

Singing at wakes died out as a general practice around the end of the last century, but lingered on in some areas until twenty years ago or so. As well as the types of songs already mentioned, psalms and carols were to be heard at wakes in a few districts[19]. Psalms were also sung at wakes and funerals in other countries; Waldron has described them for the Isle of Man[20] in the sixties of the last century; and Pennant, in his *Tour of Scotland* (1776) tells of songs in praise of the dead, which he calls 'coranichs', at funerals in that country[21].

Music and Dancing

Music was seldom played at wakes, except as an accompaniment for dancing, which was a general entertainment on such occasions. John Dunton, an English traveller, who visited Ireland in the middle of the seventeenth century, described a 'rough dance' he saw, accompanied by pipe music[22]. Thomas Dineley wrote of Irish wakes in 1681: 'At these meetings the young frye, viz. Darby, Teige, Morogh, Leeam, Rinett, Allsoon, Norah, Shevaune, More, Kathleene, Ishabeal, Nooulla, Mayrgett, Timesheen, Shinnyed, &c, appear as gay as may be, with their holyday apparell, and with piper, harper, or fidler, revell and dance the night throughout, make love and matches.'[23] Thomas Campbell, in 1778, described a wake-dance held in a barn or in a special room.[24] *Anthologia Hibernica* (1794), mentions dancing as part of a game[25]; so does Rev. James Hall (1813), who named the game at which he saw dancing, Mending the Old Coat[26]. Maria Edgeworth, in *Castle Rackrent* (1810), tells of dancing at wakes[27]. In the south of Ireland, T. Crofton Croker saw at a wake four or five young men, with blackened faces and carrying sticks, perform a dance like the English Morris Dance[28]. Brewer, in 1825, saw a merry dance to pipe music at a wake[29]; and Wood-Martin mentions what he terms an 'obscene dance', called Droghedy, as taking place at Munster wakes[30] – J. G. Prim describes it as an old-time Morris dance[31].

Thus it is evident that dancing was a normal feature of Irish wakes during the past three centuries, at least. In Chapter X, I shall mention the efforts made by some of the Irish bishops to end the custom.

Early Irish literature is almost completely silent on the question of whether the Irish people, down through the ages, danced at all. The two words in the Irish language for dancing, *rince* and *damhsa*, are both borrowed and are not native. We have plenty of evidence, however, that dancing-masters were very numerous in this country during recent centuries. I have been told by an old man that he was at a fair in Sneem, Co. Kerry, in his young days where he saw two dancing-masters perform alternately on top of a soaped barrel, vying for the privilege of teaching their art to the youth of the parish during the following year. These itinerant teachers were very popular, and from them the people learned how to dance. My friend, Fionán Mac Coluim, has told me that he heard how a dancing-master died in Liscarroll in Co. Limerick. He was waked there for a few nights to the accompaniment of much fun and music, and when it was over, the people of a neighbouring parish took the body to be waked in a similar way for two further nights in their own district. Such was the estimation in which that dancing-master, for one, was held!

It is said that even the corpse was sometimes taken out to dance! The usual dances performed at wakes were single or double reels, jigs and hornpipes, as well as sets. In the rare cases where neither a piper nor a fiddler was available, a mouth-organ or lilting sufficed.

Dancing took place at Scottish wakes too in the eighteenth century. Mrs. Skith has described a wake-dance where the floor shook so strongly under the feet of the dancers that the corpse fell from the bed among the crowd[32]. In Scotland too, Pennant (1776)[33] and Mackintosh[34] tell that the dancing at wakes was led by the relatives of the deceased. And there are many references to dancing at wakes in Scandinavia[35].

Card-playing[39]

Some play the trump, some trot the hay;
Some at macham, some noddy play.

Those two lines are extracted from *The Irish Hudibras*[36] a mock-heroic poem (on the lines of Virgil's *Aeneid*), written by James Farewell in 1689. They occur in his description of an Irish wake. Brand, in *Popular Antiquities* (1841) says that 'macham' was a type of card-game[37]. Whether it was or not, we have ample evidence[38] that cards were occasionally played at wakes in this country, especially when the deceased was old, and when the attendance at a particular wake was small. If it happened that the dead man had been fond of cards himself, his

31

friends sat around the bed to play some game which was popular locally, and a 'hand' of cards was even given to the corpse[40]; the game might also be played at a table in the kitchen. It may be said that giving cards to the corpse was done as a joke, but it will be seen later that the custom possibly had another significance. Tricks with cards were also occasionally performed at wakes.

Riddles

Young people often resorted to riddling among themselves, when they needed a rest between more formal games. It was only an interlude, however. A penalty would be imposed on the person who failed to come up with the correct answer. Also, trick questions, which involved the unusual use or pronunciation of certain words, were tossed about on these occasions[41].

Tongue-twisters

These were a common form of amusement for young people both at wakes and elsewhere[42]. They were in either Irish or English. The genre is so well-known that there is no need to give examples here. They often formed part of a more elaborate game, as, for example, *Scaoil Thart an Chearc Ghearr* (Pass the Short Hen about), which was played as follows: One end of a small stick was 'reddened' in the fire. One player held it while reciting a long tongue-twister and kept waving the stick to prevent the 'red' end from becoming black. If he succeeded in doing this, he quickly passed the stick to his neighbour, who had to repeat the same rigmarole, while keeping the burnt end from dying out. Thus it went on; each player was allowed to blow on the 'red' part during the rhyming. The player in whose hand the Short Hen 'died' had to suffer some penalty. This game was also known as *Dealán Dé, An Birín Beo* and Tom's Alive[43].

Versifying

It has been recognised from time immemorial that work of certain kinds is performed with greater ease to the accompaniment of suitable music or song (Occupation Songs, so called). We have examples of ploughing tunes, for example, and of milking and spinning songs[44]. In Conamara, it was a normal practice for groups of women, who were working near one another, to make up extempore verses as they laboured, and sing them to well-known tunes. *Óra mhíle grá*, which is still commonly sung in the Gaeltacht, was one of the best-known *formulae*. The words had, in most cases, topical application and occasioned much laughter among the listeners. As in the case of tongue-twisters and riddles, this versifying usually took place at wakes during a rest-period between games.

Repetition of Jingles

This type of entertainment, which was also carried on at wakes, differed from the saying of tongue-twisters, which has already been mentioned. Several games such as *Iasc ar Bhord an Rí* (Fish for the King's Table), The Twelve Days of Christmas, The House That Jack Built, A Fine Fat Hen, Knife and Fork for My Lord's Table, and The Crooked Crab-tree[45] involved the repetition of set lines of poetry. They varied little in the way they were played. The players stood in a circle, one of their number being in the centre. This leader would place a ring or some similar small object in the hand of the first player, who would ask him 'What is this?' 'A fat hen,' the leader would reply. The first player would then pass the object to his neighbour, who would ask the same question. The reply in this case would be 'A Fat hen and two ducks'. So the game went on until it reached the last player who was told that he (or she) had just received eight pairs of bullocks, seven pairs of boars, six pairs of red calves, five whales, four fat pigs, three grey geese, two ducks and a fat hen! The fun of the game was in the penalty imposed on any player who failed to repeat correctly, in

33

turn, his own particular jingle; it might be to kiss some fellow (or girl, in the case of a male player), or else suffer soot to be smeared on the face.

One of these wake-jingles went as follows in English:

This is the ship that came from Spain,
That carried the iron over the main,
That made the spade both stout and strong,
That dug the grave both deep and long,
That held the huntsmen, hounds and horns,
That chased the fox from under the thorns,

and so on[46]. The difficulty in repeating the words correctly caused much amusement.

NOTES

1. For accounts of Irish wakes, see Shaw Mason, *Parochial Survey*, I, 318, 595; *ib.*, II, 160, 365, 460; Mrs. S. C. Hall, *Ireland*, I, 224; *Dub. Univ. Mag.*, 8/1862, 145–157. Scottish wakes: Guthrie, *Old Scottish Customs*, 125–6, 212; MacDonald, *Echoes*, 65. Norwegian wakes: Christiansen, *The Dead and the Living*, 28. Swedish wakes: Hagberg, *När Döden Gäster*, 241; *Hwbch. des d. Abergl.*, V, 1106–.
2. Hartmann, *Totenkult*, 117.
3. *Banks of the Boro*, 57.
4. See also: Carleton, *Traits and Stories*, I, 105; Townsend, *Survey of Cork*, 90; Edgeworth, *Castle Rackrent*, 214; *Dub. Univ. Mag.*, 8/1862, 147–8.
5. *Béaloideas*, IV, 364.
6. *Spicilegium Ossoriense*, II, 239–240.
7. For storytelling at wakes, see: Shaw Mason, *Parochial Survey*, II, 460; Carleton, *Traits and Stories*, I, 105; MacDonagh, *Irish Life and Character*, 374; Mrs. S. C. Hall, *Ireland*, I, 226; Lynd, *Home Life in Ireland*, 110; Gamble, *A View of Society*, 329; Piers, *Westmeath*, 124; Croker, *Researches*, 170–1; Campbell, *Philosophical Survey*, 210; Wakefield, *Ireland*, II, 807; Charlotte Elizabeth, *Sketches of Irish History*, 146; Rev. J. Hall, *Tour*, I, 324; Lady Wilde, *Ancient Legends*, 121; *An Claidheamh Soluis*,

19/4/1909, 5; *The Shamrock*, XXXI, 180; *Dub. Univ. Mag.*, 8/1862, 147; *Saint Patrick's*, I, 725; *Ireland's Own*, XXV, No. 633, 1; *ib.*, 15/4/1903, 7; *ib.* 29/8/1936, 21; *Seanchas Ardmhacha*, I, No. 1, 124; Hartmann, *Totenkult*, 113.

For storytelling at wakes in Scotland, see MacDonald, *Story and Song from Loch Ness-side*, 156, and Mackintosh, *Notes on Strathdearn*, 34; and for same at German wakes, see *Hwbch. des d. Abergl.*, V, 1110.

8. *Hwbch. des d. Abergl.*, V, 1111.
9. See Chapter X.
10. *Westmeath*, 124.
11. 12/1794, 439.
12. *Tour*, I, 324.
13. *Researches*, 170–1.
14. *A Pilgrimage through Ireland*, 178–184.
15. Pages 156–176.
16. *Traits and Stories*, I, 105, 108–111.
17. *Béaloideas*, VIII, 129.
18. For further accounts of singing at wakes, see: Ireland: Shaw Mason, *Par. Survey*, II, 450; Mrs. Houston, *Twenty Years in the Wild West*, 121; MacDonagh, *Ir. Life and Char.*, 374; Farewell, *Ir. Hudibras*, 34; Elizabeth, *Sketches of Ir. History*, 146; Coulter, *Curious Notions*, 62; Wakefield, *Ireland*, II, 807; *Ireland's Own*, X, No. 258, 5, 17; *Ulst. Jour. Arch.*, 1856, 273; *Ulst. Review*, I, 131; *Dub. Univ. Mag.*, 8/1862, 148–153; *Salmagundi*, 22/2/1834, 18–19; *Ireland Illustrated*, 1844, 199; Hartmann, *Totenkult*, 113. Singing at Manx wakes: Waldron, *Description of the Isle of Man*, 170. At wakes in England: Brand, *Pop. Antiq.*, II, 155–168. At Scottish wakes: Pennant, *Tour in Scotland*, 112; MacDonald, *Story and Song*, 160; Mc Pherson, *Primitive Beliefs*, 125; Coulter, *Curious Notions*, 57. McPherson, *op. cit.*, 125, states that episcopal Synods in Elgin, Scotland (1621 and 1675), and in Moray (1675) condemned singing at wakes in that country.
19. See Shaw Mason, *Par. Survey*, I, 596. For the psalms sung at wakes in Sweden, see Brand, *Pop. Antiq.*, II, 143, and Hagberg, *op. cit.*, 239–246. For psalm-singing at Norwegian wakes, see Christiansen, *op. cit.*, 28, 30–31.
20. *Isle of Man*, 170.
21. *Tour*, 112.

22. Dunton (third letter), MacLysaght, *Irish Life*, 360.
23. Dineley, *Observations*, 21–22.
24. Thomas Campbell, *Phil. Survey*, 210–211.
25. 12/1794, 439.
26. *Tour*, I, 323.
27. *Castle Rackrent*, 24.
28. *Researches*, 170–1.
29. Brewer, *Beauties of Ireland*, I, clxxxv–vi.
30. Wood-Martin, *Elder Faiths*, I, 321.
    For further references to music and dancing at Irish wakes, see: Rodenberg, *Pilgrimage*, 180–1; Anon., *An Irishman at Home*, 210–1; Wakefield, *Ireland*, II, 807; Coulter, *Curious Notions*, 62; An Irishman, *Scenes and Incidents*, 97–104; *Salmagundi*, 22/2/1834, 18–19; *ib.* 26/7/1834; *Folklore Record*, IV, 100; *Béaloideas*, VIII, 133; Ó Muirgheasa, *Greann na Gaedhilge*, II, 129–132; Hartmann, *Totenkult*, 113.
31. *Jour. Kilk. Arch. Soc.*, II, 334; see also, Strutt, *Sports and Pastimes*, 310–.
32. Grant, *Everyday Life*, 132–3.
33. Pennant, *Tour*, 112. Further information about music and dancing at Scottish wakes will be found in the following: Coulter, *Curious Notions*, 57; Brand, *Pop. Antiq.*, II, 141; Guthrie, *Old Scottish Customs*, 212; Murray, *Scottish Women*, 117–; McPherson, *Primitive Beliefs*, 125; Carment, *Glimpses*, 38, 280. For accounts of the condemnation of the custom by episcopal Synods in Scotland (Elgin, 1621, 1675), see MacDonald, *Story and Song*, 155, 160, 166, and McPherson, *Primitive Beliefs*, 125–.
34. Grant, *op. cit.*, 132–133.
35. Christiansen, *op. cit.*, 28–.
    For accounts of dancing at African funerals, see: *Africa*, 12/1947, 211; *The African Missionary*, VI, 132; *ib.* XI, 62 (picture of a Nigerian funeral dance).
    According to Mansi, *Collectio*, XXV, 66, an episcopal Synod which met at Bayeux (France) about the year 1300 condemned dancing in graveyards.
36. Farewell, *The Irish Hudibras*, 34.
37. Brand, *Pop. Antiq.*, II, 142.
38. Little, *Malachi Horan*, 76.
39. *Irish Packet*, I, 423 (on the border of Texas and Mexico); Christiansen, *op. cit.*, 29 (Norway); John, *Brauch und*

    Volksglaube, 170 (Germany).
40. Hartmann, *Totenkult*, 112.
41. *Béaloideas*, XIII, 250; *Ar Aghaidh*, 2/1940, 6.
42. Lady Wilde, *Anct. Legends*, 121; Murphy, *Slieve Gullion*, 77.
43. *Ireland's Own*, LXVI, No. 1722, 14; Courtney, *Cornish Feasts*, 15–16; Gomme, *Trad. Games*, I, 256; *ib.*, II, 111, 413.
44. O'Sullivan, *Songs of the Irish*, 33–39.
45. *Anthol. Hib.*, 12/1794, 439; *Béaloideas*, VIII, 139; *ib.*, XIX, 183; *Ireland's Own*, LXV, 213; *The Bell*, III, 313; Murphy, *Slieve Gullion*, 77; Gomme, *Trad. Games*, II, 315.
46. cf. Gomme, *Trad. Games*, II, 318.

III

CONTESTS IN STRENGHTH, AGILITY, DEXTERITY, ACCURACY OF AIM; ENDURANCE AND TOUGHNESS; HARDIHOOD; AND ATHLETICS

Men of physical prowess have always been held in high esteem in every country. This was so in Ireland too, and it continues to this day – hurlers, footballers, and athletes are very popular. In times gone by, men of unusual strength received similar acclaim[1]. I well remember the attempts made by men of my native parish in Kerry, in my young days, to raise from the ground, individually, a heavy block of concrete, portion of a fallen gate-pillar. Many tried it and failed on Sunday evenings, when they had leisure. It weighed about one hundred-weight and remained firmly on the ground until a low-sized man, whom nobody regarded as being strong, succeeded one evening in raising it to his knees. From that time on, he was hailed as a champion weight-lifter, although his modesty did not allow him to show off.

As contests of various kinds formed part of the traditional pattern of sport in rural Ireland, it is not to be wondered at that they were also popular features of wakes and funerals.

Contests in Strength

One of the most usual trials of strength at wakes was known as Lifting by the Stiff Hough[2]. It had other names too, in both Irish and English. A very heavy man lay down on the kitchen floor on his back, extended his legs straight down and placed his two hands under the back of his head. He had to keep his legs stiff and unbent during the test. A second man took his stand over him, with a foot at either side of the prone one, and placed his hands underneath the backs of the knees of the other. At the first attempt, he would try to raise the prone man's body to a semi-erect position and then exert further strength to get him fully on his feet. The man on the floor was allowed to make himself feel as heavy and lifeless as possible, but he was forbidden to bend his knees.

Some of the spectators might lay bets on the contestant, whose friends did all they could to ensure that the trial was a fair one. Friends of the prone man would often try to secretly stand on the tail of his coat to keep his body near the floor, and this often gave rise to arguments and fights. The prone man, too, might get hurt if the lifter failed and allowed him to strike his head against the floor. If the lifter succeeded in his task, places might be exchanged, and so the contest went on. A burly man, with short legs, was hardest of all to lift.

Men who were winners at this type of contest in their own parish usually went to wakes elsewhere to conquer new opponents.

This kind of contest was practised on occasions other than wakes, too.

Lifting the Corpse[3]

The 'corpse' in this test of strength was not the deceased, but a very stout man who would lie down on his back on the floor, as in the preceding case. The legs had to be kept straight and rigid. Four men then tried to raise him off the floor with their thumbs, which were placed under the shoulders, right and left, and the collops of the legs, right and left, respectively. Each lifter used only one of his thumbs.

Pulling the Stick; Sweel Draughts[4]

Two men sat facing each other on the floor of the wake-house, with legs extended so that the soles of their shoes touched. A strong stick, such as the handle of a spade or pitchfork, was then laid across the tops of their shoes.

Both gripped the stick, one hand inside and one outside, and each tried, while holding his legs rigid, to lift his opponent off the floor even as much as an inch. After three pulls, places were exchanged, and the test continued similarly.

This contest was also the occasion of trickery and foul play sometimes. A man who was about to be lifted off the floor would cause his foot to slip from the opponent's shoe and thus save himself; or friends of the less skilful contestant would secretly try to tread on his coat-tails to prevent him from being lifted.

Like most other wake-tests and games, this was a usual trial of strength on other occasions, and was also practised outside of Ireland[5].

Lifting a Chair

A chair in the wake-house was gripped at the base of one of the legs by each contestant in turn in an attempt to raise it above his head. It was by no means an easy thing to do, as the old country chairs were often very heavy[6].

Breaking an Egg

An egg was held between the contestant's two hands, with the pointed ends against the palms. He then tried to crush the egg, and generally failed.

The Stronger Hand

Two men stood facing each other, with their right hands raised against each other. Pressure was then exerted by each in an attempt to force down his opponent's hand[7].

Wrestling

A man would enter the wake-house, dressed in a suit of straw, and challenge all present to 'wrestle the Connacht-man'[8]. Or, the challenger might bring in with him a stick, dressed as a strawman, and invite all comers to wrestle them both.

Contests in Agility[9]

This type of contest was popular wherever young men congregated. Space was needed on such occasions; small, crowded wake-houses were unsuitable for the purpose, as all present pressed forward to witness the contests. In certain areas, the barn, which would be empty at the end of Spring and in early Summer, was used as an arena. Here are some of the tests:

(a) A man gripped a stick with his hands at either end and tried to jump over it, without breaking his hold[10]. An open razor, edge upwards, was sometimes used instead of a stick.

(b) Twelve men faced each other in two lines, six in each row. The men in each line stood about two feet apart from their neighbours. Each player extended his two arms and gripped the hands of the man facing him[11]. Other active men at the wake then tried in turn to jump over each pair of hands in turn, down between the lines, without stopping. This was a very difficult feat to perform.

(c) The next test was known as Pell-mell outside of Ireland[12]. It was common at wakes here. Two men stood with a spade-handle or some such stick resting on their shoulders. Two others then tried to excel each other in performing acrobatic tricks on the stick, somewhat like circus performers.

(d) Two men vied with each other in somersaulting on the floor, always returning to a standing position[13].

(e) Driving the Pigs across the Bridge was the name given in South Kerry to another wake-test. Fionán Mac Coluim got an account of it in the Parish of Dromad in Iveragh. Those who arrived late at the wake-house were the 'pigs' in this case and, having been scolded for not having arrived earlier, had to submit to an ordeal as punishment. 'We must drive the pigs across the bridge,' somebody in the wake-house would say. The bridge consisted of a number of men, who stood in line behind one another, with their shoulders bent forward. The 'pigs' were then forced with blows to mount, like riders, on the backs of the others; when all had mounted, they were suddenly thrown together in a heap on the floor. This type of game was also known as *Na Bromaigh* (The Colts), *Hata Bó Dingle* and Leap-frog[14].

(*f*) Riding the Wild Ass[15] (also known as the Priest's Stirrup) was a very dangerous trick. A rope, which had a noose at one end, was thrown over one of the rafters (or roof-couples) of the wake-house. The man who wished to show his agility then grasped the other end of the rope and put one of his feet into the noose. He then pulled on the free end of the rope and tried to raise himself high enough to enable him to kick against another rafter (or couple) with his free foot. The difficulty and danger in the trick arose from the fact that one part of his body (the hands) was pulling against another (the foot), and he might easily fall on to the floor and injure his head or back.

(*g*) The wake-game known as Stealing the Goats (from Hell) in Co. Galway is described in *Béaloideas*[16]. The player grasped two sods of turf, one in either hand, and faced the floor with his hands and legs extended; only the turf-sods and the toes of his shoes were allowed to touch the floor. The player's objective was a potato which lay on the floor below his face; he had to pick this up with his mouth, without allowing his stomach to touch the floor or bending his arms or legs. This was difficult enough to do, while uninterrupted, but it became more so when he had to reply to questions during the attempt:

Questioner: Where are you going now?
Reply: Stealing the goats from Hell.
Questioner: Swear that you are.
Reply: I swear that I am.

(*h*) Another test of agility involved the lifting of a horse-shoe from the floor[17]. The shoe was placed three or four inches out from the foot of the kitchen-wall. The person who tried to pick it up took his stand about three feet from the wall, and had to pick up the shoe without bending his knees. Whenever he bent forward in making the attempt, his head would touch the wall, and he was not allowed to use his hands to help straighten himself again. This caused much amusement.

(*i*) Going Around Under a Table[18]. In this test, the player would lie face downwards on a table, catching the edges with both hands. He was then required to bring his body around under the table, between its legs, and return to his starting-point without touching the floor. His main difficulty was to keep the table from overturning in the process.

(*j*) Walking on the Legs of a Stool[19]. Many houses had long stools or forms as part of the furniture in olden times. A fairly long stool would be laid on the floor, legs upwards. The contestant had to mount the stool, placing his two hands on the front legs and his two feet on the back ones. To do the trick, he had to 'walk' around on the stool-legs with his hands and feet until he returned to his original position.

(*k*) The Donkeys and Baskets[20]. A man lay face-down on the wake-house floor. Two others sat facing each other at either side of him and extended their legs across his back towards each other. Each took hold of the other's legs. The prone man was now the 'donkey' and the other two the 'baskets'. His task was to rise up, as a real donkey would, raising the baskets on his back. Two groups of three often took part in this test, each striving to be first in completing it successfully.

(*l*) Spinning the Tin Box[21]. This was occasionally played at wakes. Each of the male players was given an even number (two, four, six and so on), while each female got an odd number. The players sat here and there in the kitchen, while a tin box, such as would hold polish, was spun in the centre of the floor by the man in charge of the game. As the box spun around, he would call out the number of some player, whose duty it then was to rush forward and catch the box before it ceased to spin. A player who failed to do so was given some penalty. This game was played, but not at wakes, in New Zealand also.

Dexterity

Games of dexterity were common at wakes, and bets were often laid on the contestants.

(a) The Tailor's Trick, or Cogglesome Curry[22]. A strong stick, such as a spade-handle, was laid on the seats of two chairs, which were placed some distance from each other. The contestant then seated himself on the stick, between the chairs, feet tucked under him, as a tailor would while working on a table. At each corner (eight in all) of the chairs, was placed a potato or a bit of turf, and the task of the player was to knock these to the floor with a small stick which he held, still keeping his balance. Experts at this game caused much amusement by pretending to sew, with the stick as needle, during the intervals between knocking down the eight objects. Another player then took up the game, and if both had succeeded in the test, the spade-handle was raised still higher on the rungs in the chair-backs until a winner was reached.

(b) Catching the Herrings. Henry Morris published an account of this Monaghan wake-game in *Béaloideas*[23]. His uncle had seen it played. A stick was placed across two chairs, as in the preceding test. The player again sat, tailorlike, on the stick between the chairs and, without losing his balance, had to pass around under the stick some small object which he held in his hand. Morris's uncle said that very few performers could do this successfully three times, without toppling.

(c) Quenching the Candle; The Bayonet Charge; Quench the Light; Putting Out the Candle; and Jenny, Will You Bake a Bit? were different names for another test in dexterity[24]. A lighted candle was placed on the floor, and two players stood near it, one behind the other. Both took hold of a four-foot long stick, which was passed between their legs, and the hindmost player would say: 'Jenny, will you bake a bit?', to which the other would reply: 'Devil a bit today, sir'. The hindmost player would then say: 'I'll put out your candle,' to which the other would reply 'If you can, you may, sir'. The hindmost player would then endeavour to knock down the candle by moving the forward end of the stick, while the player in front tried to prevent this. It is said that, so hard was it to extinguish the candle in this way, it often burned away during the various attempts.

(d) The Cockfight; The Two Uncles, and Skewer the Goose was another wake-game test of dexterity[25]. It was an attempt to imitate a real cockfight. Two men sat facing each other on the floor, knees raised. Each passed his two hands down outside his own knees and brought them up inside. The hands and knees of each player were then tied firmly with a piece of rope, and a sharp stick was put into the hands of each. These stick were to represent the spurs of the fighting cocks, and the players had to 'fight' each other, despite the difficulty of keeping erect. If a player fell to one side, he could not sit up again, and so lost the game.

(e) The Little Friar, and Shaving the Friar (Minister, Soldier) was another wake-game. A small portion of ashes was taken from the hearth and placed in a pile on the floor, with a stick, such as a match, sticking out from it on top. Five or six players sat in a circle around this, each equipped with a small stick or a knife or spoon. The first player took away a small portion of the ashes, being careful not to topple the match, and say at the same time:

Shave the poor friar to make him a liar;
Cut off his beard to make him afeard;
If the friar will fall, my poor back pays for all!

So the 'shaving of the friar' went on until some player caused the match to fall. He (or she) then had to bend down, as a penalty, while the others placed in turn various household objects (saucers, dishes etc.) on his back. He had to remain in a bent position until he guessed correctly what each object was[26]. This penalty was also imposed in another game, Sitting Bróg, which is described in a later chapter.

(f) Blind Wat; Wat in the Dark; Where Are You, Jack?, and Noreen[27]. Two players either knelt or sat facing each other, their eyes blindfolded. Each held a piece of rope or some such weapon. If the players were both girls, the first would ask: 'Where are you, Noreen?' The second would reply (in rhyme, when the game was played in the Gaeltacht); 'Here on my little stool; if you were dead, and I alive, I would be forever here on my little stool.' As soon as the second player began this reply, the first tried to guess, from the voice, whereabouts her opponent's head was, and would aim a blow with the rope in that direction. She often missed the target, as the second player forestalled her by swiftly changing the head-position. In many cases, neither succeeded in striking the opponent.

(g) The Tailors or Cluaisín (Little Ear)[28]. In this game, four or five men sat behind one another, astride a stool, all looking forward towards the leader's back. The leader held his left hand against his own right ear, to protect it. The player behind him struck him a heavy blow on the protecting hand in an attempt to knock him off the stool, and if this second player succeeded, he was thereby free to leave the game. So the game continued until only one was finally left on the stool. As may be expected, this game was rough at times, and players were hurt.

(h) The Little Comb, or Box the Tailor[29]. Two players sat facing each other on a stool, their feet tucked under them, tailorwise. While pretending to sew, each would suddenly try to hit the other with his palm, or with a pillow, to knock him off the stool.

(i) Poor Little Puss, or Poor Snipeen[30]. Again, two players sat facing each other on a stool. One of them would place his palms together in an attitude of prayer, while his opponent stroked the first player's hands gent-

46

ly, saying 'Poor Puss'. The next moment, his attitude would suddenly change and he would try to strike the opponent's hands a sharp blow; if the latter withdrew his hands quickly enough to escape the blow, the other player had then to be the seemingly prayerful one, and so the game went on.

(j) The Knee Game[31]. A player sat on a chair, knees apart, fists on knees. A second player knelt on the floor in front of him, and it was his task to bend his head between the knees of the first and withdraw it so quickly that he escaped being crushed and hit by the other's fists. If he succeeded in doing this, the other player had to take his place.

(k) Selling or Milking the Goat; Soft Water, Cold Water. This game was played in two ways. A player either sat on a stool or knelt on the floor, as if he were milking a goat. In this mouth he held a long wisp of straw. Two other players stood, one at either side of him, their trousers trussed up to the knees. The milker tugged at the straw one moment to bring out the 'milk', as it were, and the next he suddenly cut, with the edge of his two hands, against the bare shins of his companions. If they did not succeed in striking his hands at the correct moment with their own, he was free to punish them by continuing the 'milking'.

The game was also played as follows: twelve or upwards of twenty players sat in a ring on the floor, their trousers trussed up to their knees. In the centre stood their leader, stick in hand. As he looked around the circle, he would say something like 'Soft water, hard water, a clever old master, many's the shilling I won for you.' He would suddenly strike a blow of the stick at somebody's shins; but the sufferer was not allowed to defend himself – the player next to him had to strike a counterblow simultaneously at the shins of the leader; failing to do this, he himself was struck by the player beside him. And so the game went on until most, if not all, of the players, had red, sore shins.

Accuracy of Aim

Tests in this field of sport were widespread in olden times, and are still so today. That they were popular at wake-houses, too, is not to be wondered at. Here are some examples.

(a) I cannot say by what name this test was known. A stick, about two feet long, was placed erect on the floor, and a contestant took hold of it with both hands. He then bent down until his ear rested on the top of the stick, while his two legs were stretched out from him. His task then began: first to move his body around the stick about ten times, maintaining the same position; then, to rise dizzily to his feet, walk straight towards the wall, and put his finger on a spot marked there. Most players failed in this test on account of the dizziness they experienced[32].

(b) Re-tailing the Ass[33]. A rough sketch of an ass, without its tail, was drawn on the floor with chalk or some similar substance. The volunteer player was then blindfolded and whirled about a few times to confuse his sense of direction and aim. His task was to add a tail to the donkey. The various attempts to do this, as well as the ludicrous positions of the tail, caused much amusement.

(c) This test, also nameless, resembles the foregoing one. A sketch of a fox was drawn on the surface of a table, and the blindfolded players attempted to put the point of a pencil on the fox's ear.

(d) The Pig's Eye was a somewhat similar type of test. An eyeless pig was sketched with chalk on the floor. The blindfolded players, in turn, stood some distance off and endeavoured, by throwing the chalk, to put in the eyes. Most of the players failed in this, and their faces were smeared with shoe-polish as a penalty.

(e) The Ring on the Wall[34] was a game with a mischievous purpose. A ring was made on the wall with chalk or a charred stick. A player was then blindfolded, and his task was to walk towards the wall and place his finger within the ring. As he made his way towards the wall, with his finger outstretched, somebody would take the finger between his teeth and bite it!

(*f*) An egg was placed on the floor, and a blindfolded player had to locate it and try to break it with a stick[35].

(*g*) Shoot the Pistol demanded of a blindfolded player that he locate a lighted candle, which was stuck against the wall with grease, and quench it with his finger, or else suffer a penalty.

(*h*) Threading the Needle[36]. This would not be a hard task in the normal course of events, but, at wake-houses, the player had to perform while seated, tailorwise, on a bottle laid on the floor. The movement of the bottle made the task difficult.

Endurance and Toughness

Tests of endurance and the like have always been favourites with young people. Those who were hardiest and toughest in their normal occupations were also likely to prevail at sports which demanded these qualities. At wakes, similarly, many games called for hardihood, toughness and patience, as will be evident from the following examples.

Slapping[37]

This was one of the most common types of penalty imposed on players who failed in a game. The slaps were inflicted with a thick, hard, leather strap or with a piece of rope of similar quality, and usually referred to as a 'linger' or *faic*. So severe was the slapping in some games that arguments and fights resulted.

Apart from slaps as a penalty, the 'linger' was also used as a means of testing the hardihood of men at wakes. Carleton has left us a description[38] of an endurance test, called Hot Loof. In this, one player bent forward, placing his left hand, palm upwards, behind his back. A second player struck as hard as he could, with his own palm, at the upturned one, often three times in succession. The players then exchanged places, and the test went on until one of them could endure no longer, owing to the tingling and pain in his palm.

Patrick Kennedy has described a wake-game known in Co. Wexford as Watch the Light, which also involved slapping[39]. A number of men stood in a circle around a lighted candle which was placed on the floor, each holding one palm upwards behind his back. Another, holding a leather strap, walked around the circle on the outside, saying 'Watch the light', as he went. Any player who failed to keep his eyes continually on the candle was heavily slapped on the upturned palm.

Another test, which was simply called *Bualadh Bos* (Slapping), called for two groups of men, three in each group. The first player in group one bent forward, his palm upturned behind his back, and was slapped thrice, as heavily as possible, with the palm of one of his opponents. This pair then changed sides, and so the game went on until one group admitted defeat.

Slapping, if applied fairly continuously over a period, normally left palms very tender and sore, so attempts were made beforehand to forestall this suffering by rubbing the palms with either wax or heated chalk (from clay pipes). Another plan of some slappers was to smear the palms with cart-grease or tallow, then apply a coating of sand to them; a poor player who was slapped with such a palm was quickly out of the game.

Another slapping test was known in Conamara as *Faic na Lámh* (The Hand-strap)[40]. The two opposing teams stood facing each other on the wake-house floor at first; then all members of one team went down on one knee, each man placing one hand, palm upwards, on his bent knee. The leader of the other team held the *faic* or strap, which was made of leather or rope or else of a piece of wet net, twisted to harden it. With this he suddenly struck a blow at the palm of the opposing player, who tried to grip the strap as it struck his palm. If he failed to do this, the opposing leader passed the strap to his nearest comrade, who acted similarly towards his own opposite number. It continued thus until one of the opposing team was lucky enough to grasp the strap; when this happened, the teams exchanged places. High tempers and blows often resulted from this endurance test.

Carleton has given an account of a game like the foregoing, called Standing Brogue[41], the only difference being that it was a test between two players, not two groups.

Other wake-games which involved slapping of the opponent's cheeks were known as Selling the Eel and The Mulberry Tree, or Catching the Plovers.

Henry Morris has described in *Béaloideas*[42] a Co. Monaghan wake-game known as Fair Judge and Foul Judge. The two players chosen as judges sat side by side, while the players stood in two rows, one behind the other, in front of them. A player from the front row, holding his palm upwards behind his back, bent his head down on to the knees of the Fair Judge. Just as somebody struck his palm, the players got themselves mixed up, and the poor player who had been struck had to try to discover the offender. Having picked out somebody as the possible culprit, he hauled him before one of the judges (the Fair Judge always told the truth, and the Foul Judge told the opposite). If the unfortunate player failed to pick out the correct offender, he had to bend down once more to suffer even heavier blows until he guessed right. This game, Morris says, often caused trouble and fighting.

A Longford wake-game of somewhat similar character was called The Wrong Sow by the Lug[43]. As before the player who was struck had to guess who his assailant was; and if he blamed a player wrongly, the latter would lead him about the room by the ear (lug), pulling and striking it.

Other games which involved guessing who the assailant was were known as The Innocent Lamb, the Two Fools and the Wise Man, or the Three Wise Men and the Three Fools. To make the guessing still more difficult, the assailant was often totally unsuspected.

Still another slapping game was called The Cobbler and the Tinker or Soola Winka. A group of men sat in a line

51

on the floor, and lots were cast to find out which of them should go on one knee in front of them. When this had been decided, the person chosen had to go, blindfolded, on one knee on the floor, his back towards the rest, and one of his hands, palm upwards, behind his back. The leader of the game would already have given a name to each of the players and would now recite a rhyme such as:

Strike him, Cob, strike him, Léir,
Strike him, Tin, with a little care,
The Cobbler and the Tinker O!

One of the other players would strike the palm of the blindfolded man, who was then required to name his assailant, or else remain where he was. The names Cob and Léir, Tin and Céir are clearly derived from the Irish words for a cobbler (*caibléir*) and a tinker (*tincéir*). When the person responsible for the slapping was finally named, he exchanged places with the other player.

Another game, which resembled this somewhat, was known in different places by such names as Hold the Light, Candle (Light) to the Eye, and Scuddy[44]. One player was blindfolded in one eye; a second player them held a lighted candle in front of the uncovered eye in order to 'blind' it with excessive light. The semi-blindfolded man had to extend one of his hands, which was struck by somebody, and the sufferer had to try to see with his 'blinded' eye who had struck him, or else continue to suffer further punishment.

HARDIHOOD

The game *Tóin Chrua* (Hard Bottom)[45] caused much amusement at wakes. Four players were involved. Two of them took hold of two others, one each, by the neck and legs and struck their posteriors together to find out which was the harder! This would remind one of the folktale character, *Tóin Iarainn* (Iron Bottom).

Another test of hardihood was Knuckling. Two men stood out on the floor; each closed a fist and then took turns in striking his own knuckles against those of the opponent. One of them usually withdrew from the contest, and so it ended[46].

ATHLETICS

At wakes in some districts, it was customary for the young men who were present throughout the night to leave the wake-house after dawn and hold athletic contests in an adjoining field. Seán Mac Meanman has referred to hurling, jumping and wrestling of this nature at Donegal wakes[47].

Similarly, it was a normal custom for young men to engage in tests of various kinds near the wake-house, while waiting for the funeral to leave for the graveyard. 'Casting' heavy stones was one of the sports indulged in. So also were contests in jumping; the best athletes in the parish vied with one another in the long jump, preceded by a run, the long jump (or three such) from a standing position, the high jump, and the hop, step and jump. All who had gathered for the funeral became spectators, and they urged on the various athletes, as they would on other similar occasions[48].

NOTES

1. *Idrottslekar*, I, 32 (in Sweden).
2. *Idrottslekar*, I, 31–32 (in Sweden).
3. *Idrottslekar*, I, 48 (in Sweden).
4. Brand, *Pop. Antiq.*, II, 234; Sutton-Smith, *Games of New Zealand Children*, 147; Gomme, *Trad. Games*, II, 222.

5. Strutt, *Sports and Pastimes*, 194; *Idrottslekar*, I, 9.
6. *Idrottslekar*, I, 33.
7. *Idrottslekar*, I, 7; Olofsson, *Folkliv och Folkminne*, II, 288.
8. See pages 89–91.
9. Hartmann, *Totenkult*, 113.
10. *Idrottslekar*, I, 33–34.
11. Sutton-Smith, *op. cit.*, 140; Gomme, *Trad. Games*, I, 351.
12. Brand, *Pop. Antiq.*, II, 234; Gomme, *Trad. Games*, II, 383; Strutt, *Sports and Pastimes*, 323.
13. Strutt, *op. cit.*, 294.
14. Sutton-Smith, *op. cit.*, 138; Gomme, *Trad. Games*, I, 52, 327; Strutt, *op. cit.*, 488.
15. Gomme, *Trad. Games*, II, 192; *Idrottslekar*, I, 23.
16. XI, 176; *Idrottslekar*, I, 27.
17. *Idrottslekar*, I, 20.
18. *Béaloideas*, XI, 176; *Idrottslekar*, I, 18.
19. *Idrottslekar*, I, 22.
20. *Béaloideas*, XI, 176; *Idrottslekar*, I, 30.
21. Sutton-Smith, *op. cit.*, 109; Gomme, *Trad. Games*, II, 313.
22. Little, *Malachi Horan*, 76; *Idrottslekar*, I, 25.
23. VIII, 134; cf. Strutt, *op. cit.*, 503–4.
24. *Béaloideas*, VIII, 130; *Idrottslekar*, I, 11.
25. Sutton-Smith, *op. cit.*, 146; Gomme, *op. cit.*, I, 73, 85, 94, 191, 215; *ib.*, II, 215; *Idrottslekar*, I, 12.
26. See pages 118–121.
27. *Idrottslekar*, 1, 14.
28. Brand, *Pop. Antiq.*, II, 234; Strutt, *op. cit.*, 510; *Idrottslekar*, I, 41.
29. *Ireland's Own*, 27/11/1954, 15; *Idrottslekar*, I, 13.
30. *Idrottslekar*, I, 14.
31. cf. *Béaloideas*, III, 418.
32. *Idrottslekar*, I, 46.
33. Sutton-Smith, *op. cit.*, 112.
34. Gomme, *Trad. Games*, II, 46.
35. Gomme, *op. cit.*, I, 40; *ib.*, II, 390.
36. *Idrottslekar*, I, 26.
37. Olofsson, *Folkliv och Folkminne*, II, 288.
38. Carleton, *Traits and Stories*, I, 106–7; Brand, *Pop. Antiq.*, II, 250.
39. *Dub. Univ. Mag.*, 8/1862, 156–7; Kennedy, *Boro*, 74.
40. cf. *Béaloideas*, V, 231.

41. Carleton, *Traits and Stories*, I, 107; *Béaloideas*, V, 231.
42. *Béaloideas*, VIII, 134; Lady Wilde, *Anct. Legends*, 121; Seignolle, *Folklore du Hurepoix*, 323; Strutt, *op. cit.*, 501.
43. *Béaloideas*, VIII, 139; see also, *ib.*, III, 418; Lady Wilde, *Ancient Cures*, 128; Rodenberg, *Pilgrimage*, 180; *Ulst. Review*, I, 131; Brand, *Pop. Antiq.*, II, 235; Sutton-Smith, *op. cit.*, 90; Gomme, *Trad. Games*, I, 29, 188, 229–30; *Folk-Lore*, (1946), 86–87 (as a wake-game in the Ukraine).
44. *Ar Aghaidh*, 12/1936, 5 (*Cluife na Splinnce*).
45. Gomme, *Trad. Games*, I, 41.
46. Gomme, *op. cit.*, I, 98; *Idrottslekar*, I, 14.
47. *An Claidheamh Soluis*, 12/8/1911, 5.
48. *The Folklore Record*, IV, 100. Stewart, *A Highland Parish*, 158, describes how young men spent three days at athletic tests during a Scottish wake.

IV

TAUNTING AND MOCKING; BOOBY TRAPS; MISCHIEF-MAKING; HORSE-PLAY; ROUGH GAMES; FIGHTS AT WAKES AND FUNERALS

As I have already said, old-time wakes were occasions for fun and enjoyment, and every opportunity was taken to provide these. As in everyday life, certain persons were made the butt of jibes and jokes, and the better they put up with these, the shorter would be their ordeal.

Taunting and Mocking[1]

These features of wake-amusements were known by various names, according to the different districts in which they were practised. Sconcing, Scogging and Jib(b)ing were three such titles. The purpose of the ridicule was to make the recipient uncomfortable and to amuse the hearers. Although it was meant as fun, on the surface, still malice and insult were also present on occasions. Resentment at some jibe only made matters worse; the best policy for the recipient of the mockery was to take it in good part and hope that it would shortly be over.

Those who were active in this form of wake-sport were usually those who had lively tongues and a sharp wit. Two such fellows might start to mock and ridicule each other, in a half-insulting fashion, referring to some local matters in which either had been involved. Or else, such a pair would help each other in making humorous, though sarcastic, remarks about a third person who was present – some young fellow, for example, who was courting a local girl. He was made the scapegoat for the occasion, and his best plan was to grin and bear it. Another form of this entertainment was that some joker started to ridicule some fellow who was present and was aided in this by others who added further comments.

The foregoing ridicule was independent of formal wake-games, but it also entered into some of the latter. Making the Stack is one example of such a game[2]. Two players sat on the floor, with a small bundle of hay or straw between them. They pretended to be about to make a stack or rick. 'For whom will we make this?' one of them would ask. 'For Tady Ryan of Rath, and nobody else,' his companion would reply. 'Isn't he courting Julia McCarthy? I hope he'll soon give us a big night,' the first would rejoin. They would then go on to discuss Tady and Julia in a very personal way, as well as the prospective fathers-in-law; the more sarcastic and biting the references were, the more the audience enjoyed the fun. All the while the two players tossed the hay or straw about, preparing the stack for the young lovers. When they had said all they could think of and, as it were, finished the stack, two other players took over, and so the mockery continued until the players and audience had enough of it.

The relatives of the deceased had often to intervene when this form of entertainment was in danger of passing the bounds of propriety and giving rise to ill-feeling and violence, which might continue for several years.

Many formal games at wakes had for their purpose the discomfiture of the loser. *Ceist Agam Ort* (I Have a Question for You) was one of these. The leader of the game asked eight or ten players, young and old, men and women, to sit on long stools beside the wall. He had a helper, who was known as the Judge. The leader would then announce that he would ask each a question in turn; they must answer truthfully, or else suffer a penalty. The questions were generally of a personal nature – a fellow might be asked about his girl, say – and the Judge had to decide whether the reply was true or false. If a player gave an untrue reply, in the Judge's estimation, or if he (she) refused altogether to answer a question which was too personal, he had to suffer a penalty, which might cause him to blush still more than the question had done. Two or three extra players helped the leader to see that the penalties were carried out. Fights often ended this type of game.

Another such formal wake-game was known as Selling the Old Cow, The Parts of the Old Cow, the Goat, or Dividing the Goat[3]. Here the leader would pretend that he had the meat of a cow or goat or some other animal for division. He would give the head to one, as it were, the belly to a second, the tail to a third, and so on. Having thus divided the carcase, he would start to ask each of the recipients a question. 'What part of you is yellow?' he would ask the player who had received the belly; this player had to reply 'My belly', which caused much laughter. So the game went on, each question being intended to produce an answer which would raise a laugh. This was a somewhat unpleasant game, as it often descended to coarseness.

Booby Traps

Each game under this heading had as its main purpose the discomfiture of somebody who had never seen it played. He would be invited to take part, little realising what was in store for him. There were many such traps.

The Hive, or The Bees and the Honey[4] began by the leader announcing that he wished some fellows and girls to take part in this particular game. They stood in a circle on the floor. He would then pick out from the rest of the crowd somebody who was half-simple or who had never seen the game played, or was a stranger in the district. This fool, let us term him so, for convenience sake, was then asked to sit down on a box or chair in the centre of the circle. He was to be the Hive, the other players the Bees. When this had been arranged, the leader gave the order to the Bees to start their work. Round the Hive they went, humming, as bees would be on a summer day. The leader would then remark that there was little or no honey to be collected inside the house; they would have to look for it out of doors. The players in the circle would then make a bee-line for the door, humming as they went, and after a while they would return in line to the kitchen, still humming. Round the Hive they went until the leader ordered them to put the honey into the Hive. This was the crucial point of the game. Each player had taken a mouthful of water outside, and this was now poured by each on the head of the unfortunate Hive, soaking him to the skin. Once caught, this player, needless to say, was never again fooled!

This game was very popular as a wake-game throughout most of Ireland. Henry Morris got a description of it from his uncle who saw it played long ago near Carrickmacross[5].

It was a common game outside of Ireland too, but not at wakes. In England it was known as Blind Bees or Bees, Bring Your Honey[6]. Douglas, in *London Street Games*, calls it Deliver Up Those Golden Jewels.

Another wake-game was rather similar. The leader gave each player some word or phrase. The leader left the kitchen and, when he returned, each player had to repeat his own particular word or phrase. When a player said the chosen word or phrase, the leader douched him with a mouthful of water[7].

In The Coin and the Tun Dish, the leader placed a tun dish or some similar small vessel between the top of his trouser-band and his shirt. On his head would be a coin. He would then allow the coin to fall and would catch it in the vessel as it fell. He would then challenge everybody at the wake to do this trick. Someone who had never seen the trick before would stand out on the floor, and as he was about to try to get the coin to fall into the vessel, somebody would pour water into it secretly, wetting him well as a result.

The Spoon and the Porringer was somewhat similar. In this trick, the leader held a spoon in his mouth and a porringer of water on his head. He would tell somebody who had never seen the trick that he was going to get the water from the porringer into his mouth by means of the spoon. The fool would come near him to see it being done; the leader would then allow the water in the porringer to splash over him.

Listing for a Soldier was another booby trap game. Somebody who had not seen the game before was asked to come on to the floor, as a potential army recruit. Two or three men gathered around him, as if they were doctors testing his physical condition. When asked to raise his arms above his head, he did so, and a trickster in the loft above his head poured water down into his sleeves. This trick was called Submarines in England[8], but was not played at wakes there, so far as is known. A simple fellow would be invited to lie on his back on the floor, to simulate a submarine. He would have removed his coat, the sleeve of which would then be held above his eye, as if it were a periscope. As he obeyed an order to look through this, water was poured down through the sleeve on to his face.

Wetting the Flax[9] again called for the use of somebody who had not seen the game previously. As he stood unsuspectingly on the floor, a wisp of flax was placed across his mouth and a small vessel filled with water on his head. He was then led down the floor by somebody who held a lighted candle in his hand. This rogue would suddenly set the flax alight and the booby douched himself with the water while trying to escape being burned. If he happened to have a moustache or whiskers, these too were in danger!

The Masons[10] was the name applied to a game in which some players pretended to be building a wall, attended by a workman (he was the innocent booby). Some of the masons would go outside for mortar, as it were; instead, they brought back dirty water and mud, which they poured on the head of the unsuspecting helper.

Pulling a Man Up From the Ground With a Straw was yet another booby trap. A rogue who was at the wake would issue a challenge that he could lift anybody present off the floor, his only gear being a wisp of straw. Some simple fellow who did not know the game would

60

volunteer to be lifted. He would be asked to lie on his back on the floor, holding a wisp of straw in his mouth. The rogue would then pretend to try to lift him up with one hand by the aid of the straw, but, needless to say, he would not succeed. He would then use his other hand, as it were, and in this he held a fistful of ashes which he threw in the booby's face.

Stealing the Potato involved the placing of a potato in the fire-ashes by some player, who then boasted that he could steal the potato with his mouth, unknown to an observer, who again would be the booby. It goes without saying that it was a difficult task. The rogue would bend down on hands and knees in front of the potato, and the booby would also bend low to keep an eye on what he might do. The rogue would bend still lower, mouth open, as if to swallow the potato, and the booby's face went lower also. Then suddenly, the rogue, his eyes shut, would blow as hard as he could on the ashes, which entered the eyes of the booby. While the latter was busy trying to clear his eyes, the rogue took off the potato in his mouth and so won the bet.

Hiding the Spoons or Stones required three small stones to be placed on a table. A simple fellow who had not seen the game before was then told by a rogue to take the stones out of the kitchen, one by one, and hide them; he, the rogue, boasted that he would be able to tell him where he had hidden the third stone. The booby then went out twice and took great trouble in hiding the first two stones. While he was outside, a fourth stone was being secretly heated in the fire and it, (instead of the third stone, which was hidden) was lying on the table when he returned. When he took the hot stone in his hand to take it out, it burned him, of course, and he had to drop it instantly. 'That's where you hid the third one!' the rogue would then cry, pointing to where it lay on the floor.

In some districts in Ireland, spoons were used in this game instead of stones.

In the trick known as I'll Whistle You in Through the

Keyhole, a player would wager with a simple fellow, who did not know the game, that he could bring him in through the keyhole from outside by merely whistling. The booby went outside the door. The red-hot handle of a spoon was then pushed out through the keyhole, and the booby was ordered from within to take hold of it. Not knowing that it was hot, he did so and received a burn on his hand.

In playing Catching the Herrings, a man placed a pair of tongs about his own neck; the two arms of the tongs hung down along his chest. He would then bet that he could bring herrings, fresh from the salt water, down through the chimney. A booby who did not know the trick would wager against him. He was then asked to leave the kitchen for a short while, during which the two arms of the tongs were heated in the fire. When the booby returned, the other man still had the tongs about his neck as before; this man would then confess to the booby that he could not perform such a trick at all. It had already been arranged that, in case the herrings were not produced as promised, the booby would be free to squeeze the other's neck with the tongs. When he took hold of the arms of the tongs to exact the penalty, he had to let them go quickly, causing all at the wake to laugh at his discomfiture.

I'll Whistle You in Bareheaded was still another booby-trap. A rogue who knew the trick would wager with a booby that he could bring him back into the kitchen bareheaded, if the booby went outside the door. The booby would stand outside, keeping his hat or cap firmly on his head all the while, until the rogue shouted to him to come in. He would do so, still holding his headgear firmly in place, only to find that it was the rogue who was meant to be bareheaded, as he was at this stage. The obscure wording of the wager was the clue to the trick.

I'll Whistle You In With One Call[11] was another game intended to trap a person who had not seen it already. The rogue would tell the booby that, if he went outside the door, he (the rogue) could bring him back in again with only a single whistle. The booby stayed outside when he heard the first whistle, refusing to cooperate with the man within. There he was allowed to remain, for no second whistle was given, until the lapse of time, or the cold or rain, forced him to re-enter the kitchen.

What Am I Doing? was another booby trap, which was played at wakes. The rogue blindfolded himself in this case, telling the booby that he could tell what he was doing, although he could not see him. The booby would then make some strange grimace or take up an unusual attitude, asking at the same time 'What am I doing?' 'You are making a big fool of yourself,' the rogue would reply, to the amusement of the onlookers.

In order to play the trick called Firing the Ring, a circle of about a foot in diameter was drawn with chalk on the floor. Someone who did not know the trick was then blindfolded and a pickaxe was put into his hands. His task was to bring one of the points of the pickaxe down within the circle, after he had been whirled around a few times to make him dizzy. The catch was that, whether he succeeded or failed, he later discovered that the point of the pickaxe had pierced a hole in his own hat or cap which a rogue had placed beneath as he struck.

Breaking an Egg in an Empty Bag was another subject for a wager. The rogue would say that it was impossible to do; the booby denied this. It took the booby but a moment to break the egg inside the bag, only to be told that the bag had not been empty, as it held the egg. I saw this type of trick carried on in Kerry, apart from wakes.

In The Knees Trick, a fellow would ask somebody else, male or female, to sit on his lap. No sooner was the person seated than the follow would draw his knees apart, allowing the other to fall to the floor.

A somewhat similar trick was The Seat Between the King and the Queen[12]. The so-called king and queen would take their seats on two chairs, a few feet apart. A shawl or some similar covering extended from the seat of one chair to the other, simulating a third seat in between. The pair would invite a third person to sit between them, and no sooner had he (she) done so than the pair stood up, causing the third to collapse to the floor.

In England, this was a common parlour-game[13], and was known as The King and Queen of Sheba. Strutt says that it was a popular boobytrap in colleges there. Grose, too, mentions it under the name of The Ambassador, and says that it was in great vogue among sailors[14].

In another type of boobytrap, the onlookers, not an individual, were the target of the game[15]. It was played as follows. Three objects, such as stones, cups or cards, were laid on the table or on the floor. The ringleader would then announce that he would go outside the door; in the meanwhile, any member of those who remained within was free to touch any single one of the objects. On his return, the ringleader would examine closely the three objects, touch and smell them, and announce which one of them had been touched in his absence. He was always right! The whole company would be amazed at this display of special knowledge. The test was repeated several times with the same result. How was the trick – if trick it was – done? This is the solution. The ringleader had an accomplice in the audience. This accomplice would hold a pipe or cigarette in his mouth, keeping it to the right of his mouth, if the righthand object were touched, to the centre, if it were the centre object, and to the left, if it were the object on the lefthand side. One glance at the accomplice gave the ringleader his clue; the examining of the stone and the smelling of it were meant only to mystify and confuse the audience.

Satisfaction was another game which was intended to deceive the whole audience. Eight players or so would stand out on the floor, with a leader and his servant in charge. This pair would start an argument as to which game they would play, and would finally settle on Satisfaction. The leader would then order the eight players to go down on their right knees, placing their left hands on the floor. When this had been done, the servant would start an argument with the leader, saying that the players should be down on their left knees, having their right hands on the floor. After a long argument, during which the eight had to remain in their uncomfortable position, the decision might be arrived at either way. Some other order was then given to the eight players by the leader, and this was followed by a similar long-drawn-out argument between the servant and the leader. The eight players would, by this time, be quite tired of the whole affair, but they had to remain as they were. So the leader and servant continued to argue for a long time over each order, until the leader would finally ask the players if they were satisfied. They would all reply angrily that they were not even half-satisfied. 'Stay as you are then!' the leader would answer, and he and the servant went on with their pretended argument. The whole purpose of the game was to tire the players and make them angry.

Mischief-making

A story in *Béaloideas*[16] is concerned with the experience of a migrant labourer from Kerry at a wake in Tipperary. Like myself, this spalpeen knew only of wakes which were carried on with decorum and good behaviour. The wake which he saw in Tipperary was of a different kind, however. Clods of turf were thrown in the wake-house[17], and the corpse itself was not immune from violence. The Kerryman, relating his experience, told of tears falling from the eyes of the corpse when it was struck. 'A wedding should be a wedding, and a wake should be a wake,' concluded the honest spalpeen.

The Kerryman, in his day, and most of us nowadays may not like such mischievous behaviour as was carried on at wakes in olden times, but it must be stated that it was the norm, not the exception, throughout the greater part of Ireland. Unruly conduct was always the rule at the wakes of old people[18]. As already stated, this was not intended as disrespect for the corpse or for the relatives; rather was it the common traditional pattern of behaviour on such occasions. Those who were present enjoyed it, and it was stopped only if it went beyond the bounds of decorum.

As at the wake which I myself attended in Mayo over forty years ago, where potatoes were the missiles, turf-sods or portions of them (*cadhráin*) were equally used in this way over most of Ireland. Even persons who were no longer young took a hand in the 'croosting'. Besides turf, the shanks of clay pipes were also broken off by those who did not smoke and used as missiles; the targets were usually unpopular individuals or crusty old men, who were easily angered. Whatever was ready to hand would be used: potatoes, water or anything convenient. 'We'll have a night of croosting', the young folk would cry with joy, whenever they heard that some old person had died in the parish.

Other types of mischief were also carried on[19]. Pepper might be mixed through the tobacco which was distributed in clay pipes at wakes, or else it would be blown in through the keyhole of the door, causing all present to sneeze violently. When they tried to get out into the fresh air, they would often find that the door was tied firmly from the outside to make matters worse. Even the chimney might be blocked with grass-sods or a wet sack, and those at the wake would be half-suffocated before they could open the door.

Other mischievous acts included putting tobacco into the teapot, or, if it were Autumn, placing nuts in the fire (these would explode with a loud bang). Meat for the visitors was often boiled in a pot at wakes, and tricksters would look for an opportunity of stealing it and inserting an old boot or a garment into the pot instead. If the relatives of the deceased happened to be miserly and provided little food or drink for the guests, the young fellows at the wake wreaked vengeance on the stacks and ricks in the haggard before morning.

In the semi-darkness of the wake-house other pranks were carried on surreptitiously, such as pricking people with pins or needles; tying together the boot-laces or coat-tails of two persons who sat side by side; secretly fastening some old man to his chair, or sewing his coat-tails to the shroud about the corpse; suddenly extinguishing the lights in the wake-house; or leaving a player who was blindfolded during a game alone in the house with the corpse. Idle hands and high spirits provided ample means for mischievous behaviour on these occasions.

It often happened that an old person would doze or fall fast asleep at a wake as the night wore on; when this happened, he was an immediate target for some trick[20]. Stories by the hundred are told around the Irish country-side about wake-sleepers who awoke minus their beard or moustache; or else their faces would be blackened with polish or soot while they slept, or, on awaking, they would find themselves bound hand and foot, unable to move.

As already stated, even the corpse occasionally became involved through these pranks[21]. One of the commonest stories in this regard tells how the limbs of an old person who had died were so bent through rheumatism or arthritis that they had to be tied down with ropes to straighten them for the period of the wake. In the dusk-like atmosphere of the wake-house, some trickster would secretly cut the ropes, causing the corpse, as it were, to sit up, terrifying those around[22]. Or else a rogue might hide himself under the bed on which the corpse was laid out and cause it to shake from side to side, frightening everybody. Some accounts tell how such a trickster was, himself, found dead underneath the bed later. I have already mentioned how cards might be played on the bed where the body lay, or else on the corpse itself; and the corpse too would be given a hand of cards. A pipe was sometimes placed in its mouth; and occasionally it was taken on the floor to dance. These aspects of the wake will be referred to more fully later on in this book. It can be readily understood that, when rough games and horse-play were carried on in small wake-houses, it might easily happen that the bed or table on which the corpse lay would be overturned, causing the body to fall to the floor.

Young fellows sometimes found that they had not enough scope for their mischievous instincts within the four walls of the wake-house itself, and went off to neighbouring houses and farms in the darkness to cause trouble there. Unpopular farmers were the targets on these nocturnal forays. Gates would be removed from their posts and hidden; crops would be pulled up; apples or other goods would be stolen. I have heard how fellows stole some hens from a farmyard and took them to the wake-house, where they cooked and ate them. In the northern parts of Ireland where cockfighting was a popular sport, young fellows from a wake-house would steal cocks from local farms and set them to fight on the floor to entertain the wake-guests. A priest from Co. Wexford has told me about one of his uncles who had one hundred and twenty stooks of oats in a field near a wake-house. The young fellows at the wake went into the oat-field during the night and doubled up the stooks, so that the farmer thought next morning that half of his harvest had been stolen, the stooks having been reduced to half of their former number.

Rough Games and Horse-play

Many of the games played in wake-houses were rough[23]. The players were, for the most part, young and robust, and spared neither themselves nor others. Several games involved penalties on the losers, mainly consisting of heavy strokes with a strap; or else, in the hurly-burly of horse-play, similar punishment was inflicted on those who were, for some reason, unpopular[24]. Indeed, I have heard that sometimes people were hurt so seriously at wakes that their injuries affected them for the rest of their lives.

Tinkering Them Out was an example of such over-strenuous games. Two groups of men formed up within the wake-house, and each did its best to force the other out through the doorway. They pushed, struck, pulled and knocked one another until the kitchen resembled a battle-area, with furniture either broken or upset all over the place. The final paragraph in this section describes a game of a somewhat similar nature, The Fat and the Lean Sheep[25], in which political factions took part. In The Spy and in Beat Out the Bull, men concentrated on ejecting a single individual from the house. Mud, farmyard manure or dirt of any available kind were rubbed to players or thrown about indiscriminately in other games, such as The Stocking of Ashes, The Spinning-wheel, and Shooting the Buck[26]. In the last-mentioned game, a man entered the kitchen, dressed as a buck-goat (clad in an old goat-skin) and carrying a three-legged stool on his head to represent horns. A second man in the kitchen would then pretend to shoot the 'goat' with a stick, while three or four others stood ready to catch the animal when he fell. As the 'goat' fell to the floor, he toppled a dish of dirty water which was on top of the stool-legs down on anybody who was nearby.

The Clean Sheep and the Dirty Sheep was another rough game[27]. A group of men stood outside the door of the wake-house, while two players kept sentry in the doorway. The duty of the sentries was to allow some other players within to pass out through the door as sheep. Now sheep may be clean or dirty, and in this game, if the sentries did not like one of the sheep, they would give a signal to the group outside that a dirty sheep was on its way out. The unfortunate fellows who were so designated were then 'cleaned' by the fellows outside by being douched with lots of dirty water or else dipped into the cesspool of the dunghill nearby. The 'clean' sheep, friends of the sentries, escaped this attention, and were set free outside.

In other games, soot, boot-polish or some similar substance would be smeared on people's faces. Billy Booby (The Plates Trick) was an example of this. A group of men stood in line on the floor; behind them stood the leader of the game, his palms smeared with soot or polish. He acted the following words which he repeated:

I take my neighbour by the chin,
Right foot out, and left foot in;
Right foot in and left foot out,
Billy Booby, turn about.

Having finished the verse, he turned each player around to face himself; anyone who failed to turn quickly got his face blackened. The more faces blackened, the greater the fun for the onlookers, so very few escaped unscathed.

The foregoing game was played as follows also. When players had been chosen to take part, all lights in the house were quenched. Then the players, with the exception of the leader and an accomplice, went outside, each holding an empty saucer. The two inside had empty saucers also. When the leader had repeated the verse already quoted, in the darkness, both he and his accomplice each rubbed his own face with his palms. Those outside were then called in one by one, the verse was repeated, and each was ordered to run his palms to his face. When the lights were lit finally, it would be seen that all, even the accomplice, had blackened faces, while the leader's face was still clean. His was the only saucer whose base had not been secretly smeared with soot before the game began.

Still another game had to be played in the dim light of the kitchen. A player, who pretended to be very ill, would lie down on the floor and roll from side to side in great pain, as it were. Another player, as doctor, would be in attendance on him. All other players had to go outside, and were admitted one by one to enquire how the patient was. As they bent down to speak to the sick man, the doctor, from behind, would smear their faces with soot or polish. None of those who came in to sympathise was allowed to leave the kitchen until all of those outside had come in. Then, when the lights were full on again, the blackened faces caused laughter all around.

Soot was also rubbed to faces in Selling the Fish[28]. Two players, pretending to be fish-pedlars, went here and there in the kitchen, offering their wares for sale.

One of them held a saucer in which was a mixture of wetted soot; the other had a very dirty cloth. They asked each person in turn if he (she) wanted any fish. No matter what the reply was, the person did not escape; those who wanted fish were given a lump of soot to chew, and those who didn't were struck in the face with the cloth.

Fights and Factions at Wakes

It will be realised by now that there was ample cause for an occasional fight to break out at a wake, because of the rough character of some of the games, the nature of some of the tricks and the mischievous behaviour and horse-play indulged in. Fights often occurred too, both in the wake-house and outside, without any apparent reason; they seem to have been started intentionally in many cases to pass away the night.

Faction-fighting was very common at fairs and such gatherings of men, especially in the eighteenth century. There are many accounts both in print and in popular memory of the Carabhats and Seanavests of Munster, as rival factions; of the Three-year Olds *versus* the Four-year Olds; of the Dáithíneachs and the Gearaltaigh (Fitzgeralds); and of many other groups who fought one another, wherever they met, year in year out. Small wonder then that the wake-house often became the arena for outbreaks of violence of this kind.

In the north of Ireland, the Molly Maguires, a very powerful organisation, went in groups to local wakes, looking for an occasion to fight. The Mollies would take part in certain games with the sole intention of beating up some man who had refused, for some reason, to join their ranks. The Fenians, too, and the White Cockades sought each other out at wakes. If a group on either side lost in a particular wake-game, they had to leave the kitchen, only to be attacked outside in the dark by some of their rivals. Those who suffered in this way would make sure to be at the next wake in the district to get revenge. Thus bad blood was engendered between the par-

71

ties until the passage of time brought their existence to an end.

As in the case of the Molly Maguires, who punished those who would not join them, so too it happened with other factions. They would go to a wake and, in the course of the night, their captain would shout that the house or barn, wherever the crowd was, had become too hot and needed ventilation. All present would be ordered to go outside. As the people passed out through the doorway, sentries posted there by the captain would give a signal to their comrades outside that a particular sheep (person) was fat or lean. The lean sheep were those who had refused to join them, and they paid dearly for it outside in the yard. Henry Morris, who has described this type of activity, says that wake-games were on their way out when these factions were active, and that the clergy did all in their power to end this feature of wakes[29].

Fighting and Strife at Funerals[30]

There is evidence to show that the relatives of the deceased looked forward to fighting at the funeral, and were very dissatisfied if none occurred. A story is told about the funeral of an old man in the northern part of Leinster. After a quiet, peaceful funeral, the mourners were about to leave the graveyard when the son of the dead man shouted:

'This is a sad day, when my father is put into the clay, and not even one blow struck at his funeral!'

As he ended his complaint, he delivered a blow at the man who happened to be nearest to him. In a few moments, fights were taking place all over the graveyard, each man taking on his neighbour. When the demands of the occasion had been met, the dead man's son called for a truce, and both he and everybody else went home satisfied.

Later on in this book, accounts will be given of the attempts made by the clergy to end this practice, until it ceased altogether.

1. *Béaloideas*, VIII, 129–130; Mrs. S. C. Hall, *Ireland*, I, 224; *Dub. Univ. Mag.*, 8/1862, 146; *Ireland's Own*, XIX, No. 480, 4; Hartmann, *Totenkult*, 113.
2. See pages 78, 88–89.
3. Ó Ruadháin, *Pádhraic Mháire Bhán*, 120; cf. Gomme, *Trad. Games*, II, 114.
4. Little, *Malachi Horan*, 76.
5. *Béaloideas*, VIII, 132, 139.
6. Opie, *Lore and Language*, 296.
7. Gomme, *Trad. Games*, I, 120; Hartmann, *Totenkult,* 117.
8. Opie, *Lore and Language*, 296.
9. Gomme, *Trad. Games*, I, 120.
10. Gomme, *Trad. Games*, I, 120.
11. *Ireland's Own*, 1/8/1917, 80.
12. Strutt, *Sports and Pastimes*, 396; Gomme, *Trad. Games*, I, 59; Brand, *Pop. Antiq.*, II, 266; Sutton-Smith, *op. cit.*, 107.
13. Opie, *Lore and Language*, 295; Strutt, *op. cit.*, 505.
14. Opie, *op. cit.*, 295.
15. Gomme, *Trad. Games*, II, 187; cf. Sutton-Smith, *op. cit.*, 107.
16. *Béaloideas*, IX, 276.
17. Hartmann, *Totenkult*, 113.
18. Dineley, *Observations*, 34–35 (notes by John O'Donovan).
19. Ó Ruadháin, *op. cit.*, 121; *Ireland's Own*, 15/4/1903, 7; Little, *Malachi Horan*, 71.
20. Ó Ruadháin, *op. cit.*, 123; *Ireland's Own*, 15/4/1903, 7; Dunton (third letter: MacLysaght, *Irish Life*, 360).
21. Murphy, *Slieve Gullion*, 70; Coulter, *Curious Notions,* 58; *Father Matthew Record*, XXII, 215; Hartmann, *Totenkult*, 113. For a Scottish story (common in Ireland also) about a rogue who was found dead in the coffin from which he had removed the corpse), see Henderson, *Notes*, 28–47. See also Christiansen, *op. cit.*, 32–34 (a Norwegian story), and Puckle, *Funeral Customs*, 61.
22. Hartmann, *Totenkult*, 113.
23. Carleton, *Traits and Stories*, I, 106; Little, *Malachi Horan*, 71; *Béaloideas*, XIII, 250; *Seanchas Ardmhacha*, I, No. 1, 124.
24. Hartmann, *Totenkult*, 113.

25. See page 72.
26. Kennedy, *Boro*, 74–75; *Dub. Univ. Mag.*, 8/1862, 157; Hartmann, *Totenkult*, 115–6.
27. cf. *Ulst. Review*, I, 131.
28. *The Bell*, III, 313.
29. *Béaloideas* X, 285.
30. Rodenberg, *Pilgrimage*, 182; Mrs. S. C. Hall, *Ireland*, I, 231; *Béaloideas*, VIII, 138; *ib.*, X, 285; Le Fanu, *op. cit.*, 35; *Ireland's Own*, IV, No. 95, 19; *ib.*, LXIII, 225; *ib.*, 24/10/1936, iii. For accounts of fights at Scottish funerals, see Mackay, *op. cit.*, 464; MacDonald, *Story and Song*, 167; Puckle, *op. cit.*, 63.

V

IMITATIVE GAMES

Games played by children, as well as the so-called parlour-games of adults, are in many cases imitations or by-forms of everyday human activities[1]. Similarly with plays of the theatre. All are meant as entertainment. Wakes in olden times, and up to our own day almost, were, as we have seen, occasions for gaiety and amusement in most cases, and games which simulated human affairs formed a large part of the wake-repertoire[2].

The Mock Court, or The Police Game[3]

Eight or so of the players remained in the kitchen, while everybody else went outside the door. Those who were inside then divided themselves up according to their duties in the game; one would act as judge, two as lawyers; one as court-clerk, and three or four as policemen. The police would then go outside and drag in somebody as prisoner, while the others pressed in also to hear the case being tried. The judge took his seat, and the clerk read out the name and address of the prisoner, as well as the offence with which he was being charged. The trial then proceeded as it would in a legal court, one lawyer prosecuting, the other defending. The main source of the fun, apart from the charge itself, was to be found in the sly references made by both counsel to the private affairs of some of those present, who were dragged into the case. These mischievous, though irrelevant, hints caused great laughter, as they were understood by all. Having heard the evidence, the judge announced his verdict, which was witty and light or severe, according to how he regarded the defendant. The police had then the task of seeing that the verdict was carried out; if guilty, the defendant might be handled roughly as punishment, or even doused nine or ten times in a tub of water. If the first trial produced a good deal of amusement, a second or third would follow, until all were tired of the game.

A somewhat similar game, which involved a court-case, was the following. A man lay down on the floor, feigning illness, and a doctor would be sent for. The doctor arrived into the kitchen on horseback, the horse being two fellows clad in straw to resemble an animal. The horse would be a very wild one and, in the course of prancing around the kitchen, the doctor would be thrown down on top of the sick man on the floor. When examined, it would be found that both the patient and the doctor were dead, and the two who played the part of the horse would be tried for causing their deaths.

Building the Ship[4]

John L. Prim has left us a rather garbled account of the way in which this game was played at wakes in Kilkenny over a hundred years ago[5]. He mentions how the keel was laid first, followed by the prow and stern of the ship; then a woman, who was taking part in the game, would raise the mast with some gesture and speech that convinced Prim that the game had its origin in pagan times. His account is so unclear that it would be difficult, for want of additional details, to imagine how the game was really played.

Again, Henry Morris has said that his uncle had seen a somewhat similar game played about one hundred years ago in Co, Monaghan[6]. It was a lively game, with lots of activities going on, he said; the only part he could re-member was the tarring of the ship (soot being smeared on somebody). Morris said that the game died out in Farney, Co, Monaghan, before the year 1880.

A Co. Galway man has described the game to me, as he saw it played there. Three men sat down astride a stool, one behind the other, all facing in the same direc-tion. The man in front was the prow of the ship; the man in the middle, the body of the ship; and the third man the stern. A fourth player stood on the floor beside them; he was the builder of the ship. He would ask the company for a hammer or sledge, which he needed for the work, and he got it – a hard sod of turf, a piece of turnip, or something like that. Having got the implement, he would walk around the stool, talking loudly to himself about his accomplishments as a ship-builder. He would then insert the right hand of the centre man under the right arm-pit of the man in front, and continue to walk around the ship, striking hard blows with his hammer on the three, as he went. He would next put the left hand of the centre man under the left arm-pit of the first man, striking blows all the time to make things firm. He then placed the legs of the hind pair around the body of the person in front of each, hammering away to keep the timbers from splitting. The trio would then have to lie back, as far as they could, and the builder would start to raise the mast. This part of the game was often obscene.

Prim has also mentioned a game called Drawing the Ship Out of the Mud, but he does not describe it[7]. It may have been part of the foregoing or, at least, related to it.

Building the Bridge[8]

Twelve men or so stood out on the floor and formed into two lines of six each, facing one another. Each man took hold of the two hands of the man opposite, thus forming the bridge from which the game took its name. The bridge had now to be tested for strength. Another player mounted on the crossed hands and walked to and fro along them. Finding no apparent fault with its construction, he dismounted. Somebody would them suggest that the bridge be tested to see if it would take a flood of water through its eye. This would be done by some rogue who sluiced the legs and feet of the players with a bucketful of dirty water.

Making the Stack

A description of this imitative game will be found in Chapter Four (p. 57). It occasionally formed the introduction, as it were, to the game known as Selling the Old Cow (Meat), p. 58.

Making the Poteen

This game, 'as well as being imitative, may also be regarded as a booby-trap. Somebody who had not seen it played previously would be asked to sit on a chair or stool in the centre of the floor. He would be, as it were, the still. The man who was working the still would walk fussily around him, getting ready for the work, while some others remained outside the house to keep an eye out for the police or 'Revenue men'. As the busy preparations were at their height within, the watchers would rush in to say that the police were coming. Speedy action was now necessary; the first thing to be done was to hide the still outside in the dark. The stiller gave this order to his helpers, and they set to work with a will. Pity the poor still! The innocent fellow who simulated that was dragged out into the darkness and flung headlong into the cess-pool of the dung-hill or some equally unpleasant hiding-place, from which he had to extricate himself without light or help[9].

Coining the Money

This again was a booby-trap and was played in much the same manner as the previous game. Counterfeit money was to be coined, as it were, and some innocent fellow was got to sit in the middle of the floor to represent the mint. The players circled around him, chanting 'Coin the money! Coin the money!' until somebody rushed in from outside to say that the police were approaching. The mint had now to be hidden as quickly and as disagreeably as the still in the preceding game.

Sledging

Another booby-trap of an imitative nature. The master-smith and his helpers announced that they had to make some plough-'socks', or horseshoes or something like that. A man who had no experience of the game was asked to sit in the centre of the floor to represent the anvil. As soon as the victim was seated, the master and his apprentices began to thump him with their fists, as hammers, chanting in time with the blows:

Strike him, strike, strike together!
Strike, strike, all together!

Having pummelled the anvil well for a time, one of the apprentices would suddenly shout that the anvil was on fire! It had to be taken out quickly lest the forge be burned. The poor anvil was taken hold of by three or four strong fellows and dumped into the cess-pool outside, or else was douched with buckets of water[10].

The Kiln on Fire[11]

In this game, players simulated a miller and his men drying corn. The floor represented the kiln. The miller would order his men to bring in sacks of corn to put into the kiln. Each man went outside and came back with a man on his back; this process went on until some twenty men, as sacks, were lying in a heap on the floor. They were left there for a while to dry, as it were, and were then turned, those underneath being placed on top. When this had been done, and the process of drying the corn was progressing well, one of the workmen would suddenly shout that the kiln was on fire. The miller and his helpers would rush to pour buckets of water on the sacks, drenching all who were heaped on the floor, especially those on top. In some areas, only two players took part, the miller and his daughter.

More Sacks on the Mill[12]

This game was also based on milling. One player would bend down and another would mount on his back. 'More sacks on the mill!' the miller would shout, and other players would get on top of the first two. By this time, the 'sack' underneath would be well loaded, and the game ended by his throwing the others down on to the floor.

The Deaf Miller[13]

A player (the miller) sat on the floor, mixing soot and water in a dish with a stick. As he worked, he carried on a conversation with himself, his remarks causing great laughter among the audience. One of his mill-hands would enter, carrying another player, as a sack of corn, on his back, and would tell the miller that the sack was to be ground. The miller would pretend not to be able to hear him, owing to the noise of the mill, and would finally order the helper to lay the sack down behind him. When five or six sacks had thus been deposited behind the miller, who all the while continued to mix the soot and water (to simulate grinding) and keep up his remarks in a loud voice, the helper would shout that the mill was on fire. The miller would have no trouble in hearing this and would throw the sooty water over his shoulder on top of the sacks behind his back, to quench the blaze.

Grinding the Cáiscín

This game also was based on work carried on in a mill. Its main purpose was to pour ridicule on some two persons who were present at the wake. Two players sat on the floor, a dish between them to represent the cáiscín (kiln-dried grain) which they were supposed to be grinding. In the course of their conversation, it would be revealed that they were doing the work for some fellow and girl at the wake, who were known to be lovers. The fun arose from the witty and caustic remarks made by the millers about this couple, their relatives, and their affairs.

80

Games of this kind were very common at wakes in the days when mills were to be found all over the country.

Lifting the Old Nag[14]

A heavily-built man would hobble into the kitchen, pretending to be an old, foundered horse, and throw himself down on the floor, grunting and complaining. Some players would gather about him, and he would ask them to raise him to his feet. Two or three would attempt this and would fail; others would come to their assistance, but even nine or ten would not be able to lift the nag. The leader of the game would then order them to remove their coats. They did so, throwing aside the coats here and there, and started to lift again, straining every muscle, but to no avail. The nag was too heavy. The leader would then order them to remove other garments, and when they had finally got rid of their socks, they would succeed in their task. At this point, some mischievous fellow would quench all the lights in the wake-house; the others would let the nag collapse on to the floor and, in the darkness, set about finding their clothes, which would have been hidden away by members of the audience. Rough-and-tumble searching went on until the lights were restored, and the game was over.

The Drunken Man

A stout man would stagger into the wake-house, pretending to be drunk. He would take off his coat and throw it aside to somebody; to another he gave his hat, to a third his waistcoat. So he continued to rid himself of his property: a bottle of whiskey, a glass, a stick, and so on. During this time, another player would keep hold on him, to keep him from falling, as he reeled about, singing some unintelligible song. He would end by asking to have his coat and the other things back, but no sooner would he receive them than he would throw them away again. Members of the audience would put the various things ahide, and, if the helper of the drunken man, could not recover them, he was beaten with a strap by the leader. The search for the garments and other objects led to much rough play, during which the drunken man would collapse on to the floor. The leader would ask various men in the audience in turn to raise him up; this was easily done if he happened to have whiskers, but, if they failed to lift him, the strap was applied vigorously.

Drawing the Bonnavs

A player sat down on the floor with his back against the wall. A second sat between his two legs, a third between the two legs of the second, and so on until six or eight players sat in line, each gripping the man in front of him firmly. These players were the bonnavs (young pigs). Three or four other players would now catch hold of the legs of the bonnav furthest from the wall and try to pull him away from the others. The bonnavs held on to one another as tightly as possible, and the game continued until the line either held intact or was pulled to pieces.

Cutting the Timber

A man lay down across the threshold of the kitchen, feet outside, head within. He was to represent the saw. Two players now took hold of his feet outside, while two others caught his head and shoulders in the kitchen. They pulled against one another, forward and backwards, as if they were sawing wood, until one pair proved too strong for the other.

The Porpoises

In the old days, it is probable that this game was played only along the sea-coast. A player assumed a stooping posture, and others leaped over his back like porpoises in the sea. It was a rough game.

Sowing the Seed

The seed in this game was the dust and cobwebs which were to be found on the rafters of old houses. Three or four players would enter the kitchen, each having a sweeping-brush, and round the kitchen they would go, brushing the dust and cobwebs down on top of those who sat there.

The Dry Barber; The Shaving Game[15]

In The Shaving Game, the leader and his assistants went through the crowded kitchen of the wake-house to find out who needed a shave. They would pick on somebody whom they might dislike for some reason, and drag him out to sit on a chair in the middle of the floor. The barbers then gathered about him and started to rub water, in which many kinds of dirt had been mixed, to his face and head. He was powerless to resist or escape. Two would then begin to shave him with bits of stick or something, as razors. The shaving was, needless to say, an ordeal in itself, and it was finished by drenching the victim with water to get rid of the soap!

For The Dry Barber, bits of paper, with numbers on them, were put into a hat or box. Whoever chanced to pick out the highest number had to sit on a chair in the middle of the kitchen to be shaved by the barber, who was the man who had drawn the next highest number. The barber donned his apron; he had two assistants. The customer on the chair, as well as the three barbers, all filled their mouths with water as a preliminary but did not swallow it. The three then started to lather the customer, as it were, trying as hard as they could to make him swallow the water in his mouth. They pressed his cheeks towards this end, and, if he did swallow it, they douched him with the water in their own mouths. It was 'dry shaving' with a vengeance!

Thatching the Stacks

The victim in this game was either somebody who had not seen it played previously, or else some person against whom a grudge was held. He had to sit on a chair on the kitchen-floor, representing the stack which required to be thatched. Two thatchers went to work on him, rubbing and stroking him, to remove, as it were, any loose straws, moving around him all the time. When he least expected it, they would strike him hard on the head and elsewhere, pretending that they were flattening bumps on the surface of the rick. This was a very rough game, and many people disliked it on that account, as little mercy was shown to the unfortunate man on the chair.

Games of Buying and Selling[16]

Many wake-games were based on everyday buying, selling and bargaining. The animals, supposedly on sale, were, in most cases, horses, sheep, asses or pigs. Hence such names as Selling the Colts, Selling the Pigs, and so on.

In one such imitative game, two players took the main parts, one the seller, the second the buyer. Other players would be driven like animals into the kitchen; they were sometimes covered with hides or skins, and were supposed to be for sale. The buyer would start off by pretending to examine each animal in turn, as would his counterpart in real life, beating them with a stick and making sarcastic comments on some. A bargain would be finally made after much argument; then the animals had to be marked, as sold. Mud or dirty water was used unsparingly for this purpose. The seller would then ask for his money, only to be told that the buyer had none; he hoped, however, that his friends would help him. His friends among the audience would turn out to be as impoverished as himself. Argument and fighting would then break out between both sides, and the animals did little to lessen the tumult.

Selling the Colts required all the men, except three, to leave the kitchen. When only these remained within, two of them took their stands at either side of the closed door, while the third stooped down inside the threshold. A player (representing a colt for sale) would then be admitted through the opened door (which was immediately closed), forced down on to the shoulders of the central man, and soot would be liberally smeared all over his face. The pair at either side then acted as buyer and seller, arguing about the proper price for the colt; when agreement was reached, the colt was set free inside the kitchen, and another colt was admitted and similarly dealt with[17].

In Conamara, a game called *Ceannuigheachaí* (Buyers) was played at wakes[18]. Each of two men, acting the part of pedlars, took a boy on his back, to represent his pack. Both carried sticks, and wandered aimlessly around the kitchen, neither pretending to notice the other. When one of them had left the kitchen, the other would ask the company if they had observed another pedlar around the district; if they said that they had, his advice to them was not to buy any needles or pins from him – his own were much superior! The wares of the rival were worthless, he assured them. The other pedlar would quickly return, and as soon as they caught sight of each other, a fight started. The onlookers too would get involved on either side, and the kitchen became a battlefield until peace was restored.

Selling the Fish[19], which was intended to give an opportunity to smear sooty water on people's faces, has already been described.

Doctoring[20]

Games in which doctors and patients were imitated were played in different ways. One such way resembles somewhat the game called Frumso Framso, which will be referred to later. The so-called patient took his seat on a chair in the centre of the floor, complaining about his pains and aches. A doctor would be summoned, and after examining the sick man, would announce that his illness was caused by his not being married! So a girl would be hauled out from the audience, and the leader in charge of the game would ask them both were they willing to marry each other. The man would say he was, but the girl would say no. The man would then leave the scene, and the girl became the patient, and so the game went on.

In another doctoring game, everybody had to leave the kitchen, except two players who represented doctors. A sick man would come in from outside and would be put lying on his back on the table, where the doctors examined him well. The 'cure' was ready to hand – soot was rubbed all over the patient's face, and he was then hidden in some dark corner of the kitchen, where he could not be seen by other patients who followed. Lights were kept very low throughout this game until the end; then all the patients vied with one another in the blackness of their faces. See also *Béaloideas*, VIII, 132.

Downey

This game was played as follows in Co. Galway[21]. A man lay down on the floor, pretending to be dead, and two other players stood over him, keening (in Irish):

> We will keen Downey, and we'll mourn him;
> If we don't keen him, who will instead?
> Downey long, and Downey short,
> And Downey nine miles over beyond the short swamp!

Round the keeners went, expressing their grief:

> Poor Downey, what a pity that you're laid low!

Four men would then raise Downey on their shoulders to take him to the graveyard. As they were about to leave the kitchen with their burden, Downey would come to life and ask them for a drink! A bucketful of water would be handed to Downey, who would dash it on top of those who happened to be within range.

The method of playing this game varied from district to district. Sometimes, when Downey lay down dead on the floor, the other players followed the traditional custom of standing around the corpse, keening and praising him, each in turn. If any of the keeners failed to do their job properly, Downey himself would rise up, bearing a strap or piece of rope in his hand. He would give each culprit a second chance to keen and praise him as he deserved; failing in this, punishment would be meted out by Downey with the strap or rope[22].

Postman's Knock

This wake-game was known by various name in Irish: *An Post; Buachaill an Phoist; Ag Rith an Phoist; Cleas na Litre*[23]. It was a well-known parlour-game in this country, as well as in England, in former years, and is now played mainly by children.

At wakes, it took either of two forms. One player would go outside, while two others stood, armed with leather straps, at either side of the closed door. When a knock at the door was heard, the sentries would enquire who was there. 'The postman,' answered the person outside. 'What do you want?' he would be asked. 'I have a letter for so and so', the postman would reply, naming some man inside. The sentries would order the man who had been named to go outside, and the postman would enter. After a few moments the man outside would knock at the door and, when asked what he wanted, would say that he had a letter for a certain girl. This girl would be sent out to him, and the man would come in. The game went on in this way, but it is said that many of the couples outside would go off courting.

Another way of playing Postman's Knock started with each man being given an even number, each girl an odd number. In the same manner as before, the postman outside the door would shout that he had a letter for, say, Number Four; the man who had this number would go outside, and the postman came in. Number Four would then shout that he had a letter for, say, Number Seven, and she would go out for it. As already stated, some couples would not take any further part in the game, and a search would be made for them.

Dividing the Meat[24]

This game of imitation had about a dozen different names in the Irish-speaking districts, which covered the greater part of the country in former centuries. The name in each case gave a clue to the kind of meat or the kind of animal whose flesh was supposed to be divided (an old cow, a bullock, a bull, sheep or lambs, rams, goats, geese, and so on). It was played in two mainly different ways, one rather simple, the second more complicated.

In the simple version, a man, who had a sheep (or other animal) to sell, would enter the wake-house, dragging another player after him to represent the animal. The seller and some buyer would start off bargaining, each as tough as the other, until finally agreement on the price was reached. The buyer would then knock the animal on to the floor and pretend to draw its blood. He would then take off the hide and cut up the carcase. He would then pretend to offer for sale imaginary portions of the meat to different persons in the company, commenting wittily and sarcastically on both the meat and the person to whom he offered it. For example, he might pretend that a certain part of the carcase had already been set aside for some man in the parish, who was not present at the wake; this man might be the butt of many jokes among his neighbours, and the seller raised many laughs by his remarks about him. He would then ask some young man at the wake to, as it were, take the meat in question to the house of the absent man; the fellow would hoist it on to his shoulder, in mime, and leave the house. He would quickly return, however, shouting and complaining that he had been attacked and robbed of the meat. The real fun then began. A few men at the wake would be accused, in turn, of the robbery, and charged with having taken the meat for their girls or their prospective fathers-in-law. This continued for some time, causing much amusement. Searchers would be sent out to recover the meat, but, of course, came back later, saying that they could not find it.

The second way of playing this game was more involved. A player scattered some straw on the kitchen-floor, pretending that it was a crop of oats which was ripe for cutting. He would call for a *meitheal* of helpers, and there would be no delay in getting them. The helpers would then get busy with the straw, reaping, binding and stacking it. They conversed and laughed as they worked, until the stack was, as it were, finally made and thatched, ready for the winter. They would then ask the farmer for some reward for their labours. While this was being attended to, another player, representing a bull, approached the imaginary stack and knocked it down with his horns. The farmer and helpers would notice what damage had been done behind their backs, suspect the bull, who had hidden by this time, and search the kitchen for him. When he was caught, the angry farmer would call for two butchers to kill him. This would be done in mime, as before, and the farmer would start to divide the meat among those present, making witty and sarcastic remarks as he went about. He would offer meat to some hungry-looking farmer, saying that it was a long time since he had tasted any, on account of his miserliness. As the meat was being divided in this manner, still another player would enter the kitchen, his head covered with a sack so that he would not be recognised. He would ask the farmer for meat for the fathers of some pair of lovers, making biting, athough still humorous, remarks about the two men in question. This would raise many laughs. The game ended as before by the meat being stolen outside, as it were, and a futile search being made for it.

Sir Soipin; Mac Soipín; Nuala and Dáithí

Suits of straw and disguises of various kinds were worn by the players in certain imitative games[25]. They had a double purpose: to suit the part and to prevent recognition by the audience.

Anthologia Hibernica[26] in 1794 made mention of a game called Sir Sop, or The Knight of Straw[27], in which it is probable that the players, or one of them at least, wore a suit of this kind. John O'Donovan, in his notes to Thomas Dineley's account of his tour of Ireland in 1681, described how a player, taking the part of a priest in a wake-game in Co. Kilkenny, seen by O'Donovan, wore a straw-suit. Anthony Raftery, the Mayo poet, in a poem describing how the storm had swept the roof off a house, says of the owner that 'he resembled Sir Soipín dressed up in a wake-house[28]'.

In the game known as Nuala and Dáithí[29], two players left the wake-house and dressed themselves in straw in the barn or haggard. The player who represented Dáithí, the man, then returned, a heavy pedlar's pack on his back and a thick straw-rope in his hand. He went through the crowded kitchen, pretending to search for his wife, Nuala, talking to himself as he went. But Nuala was not to be found. She would soon come in, however, clad in straw like her husband, and carrying a similar pack on her back. Both packs were filled with thorny furze, and both players rubbed them against as many of the audience as they could. Nuala carried a stick, but this would not prevent her from taking the floor in a dance with Dáithí. As they whirled around to the strains of the music, Nuala would suddenly pretend to fall to the floor in a faint. Dáithí would then be ejected from the kitchen, and a doctor would be summoned. After examining her, the doctor would prescribe a drink of water for the patient. As may be expected, Nuala, instead of drinking the water, dashed it all over the company. She would then call for her husband and, when Dáithí entered, he would embrace her and both began to dance once more. They would start to complain that they had not enough space for their dance and set about driving everybody from the kitchen. When the house was in an uproar, both Dáithí and Nuala would be thrown out into the yard, and the game was over[30].

This game was known by several names in the Irish language: *An Stail Bhreac, Capall an tSúis, An Láir Bhán, An Mhuc, Pin Mór* and *Mac Soipín*[31]. It was played in a rough, robust fashion. A man would enter the wake-house, dressed to represent a horse or some other animal. On his shoulders he wore a wooden head, like that of a horse, and his body was covered with a straw mat or a sheet. From the front of the head there extended a sharp spike, such as a long nail or an awl. Two other players led him in, kicking and prancing wildly like an untrained colt, and led him here and there around the kitchen. As he went about, he pricked with the spike people here and there, especially those whom he did not like. As people tried to get out of his path, the house was soon filled with screams and shouts and laughter. Quarrels and fights often resulted, as may be expected. In some areas, a second player came in mounted on the Speckled Stallion, singing an Irish song as he was carried about[32].

It may be mentioned that fellows disguised similarly as horses went from house to house in Kerry, for example, on St. Stephen's Day[33]. This had nothing to do with a wake-game, however, though the name, The White Mare, was used on both occasions.

The Hatching Hen; The Old Hen; The Turkey-cock; Feeding the Crane[34]

This game, known in different areas by the above names, resembled the foregoing one, but, instead of an animal being represented, a bird was featured. The leading player entered the wake-house, disguised in straw or other material. His head was made up to simulate a bird, the beak being formed by the point of a reaping-hook or a wooden splinter, which protruded from his face. He pretended to be ravenously hungry. Some mischievous fellow would try to relieve his pangs by taking somebody's hat, placing a fistful of corn in it, and laying it on the floor in front of the bird. The latter ran towards the food as quickly as he could and tried to pick up the grains with his beak; his main purpose, however, was to damage the hat as much as he could with the pointed spike. He would then rush about the kitchen, glug-glugging as he went, pecking at everybody, especially at those to whom he bore some grudge. In some areas where this game was played, the mother-bird would be followed about by her brood of young ones, who caused more trouble than did their mother! Again, it is said that fights often resulted from this rough game.

The Pedlars[35]

This game resembled that in which Dáithí and Nuala were characters. So far as I have been able to ascertain, it consisted of two players, an old pedlar and his wife, coming to a house to seek lodgings. On being refused, they would attack the people of the house. And even when they were admitted, peace did not follow, as the pair would start to quarrel with each other. The main purpose of the game, apparently, was to cause as much rough-and-tumble as possible.

Counterfeit Matchmaking

Financial considerations, rather than romantic love, played a most important part in rural marriage arrangements in Ireland down through the centuries. Matches were made at fairs, markets and in the houses of the young couple, where the dowry and other matters were fixed. This custom still continues to a certain extent and forms the economic basis of many country marriages.

It is said that courting and arranging matches were common at wakes too[36]. A mother who had a marriageable son might see a woman who had an equally marriageable daughter, and would try to get close to her at the wake to slowly introduce the question of a match for the pair. It often had a fruitful result.

Apart from this serious aspect of matchmaking[37], a

number of wake-games were based on the arrangement of marriages, as witness the following[38].

The Nine Daughters; The Tinkers[39]

In this game, a man sat on a stool on the floor, surrounded by nine girls, who represented his daughters. Nine men would enter, one by one, and ask for the hand of one of the daughters. Each man would have his own particular trade, as it were. If the first happened to be, say, a cobbler, he would enter, singing:

Here comes a cobbler so neat and so fine,
Coming to court your daughter divine.

The father of the girls would question him about his trade and would seem quite dissatisfied with the answers. He would then sing:

I'll set my nine daughters down by my knee,
And no old cobbler will get one from me.

Thus the father would refuse to give a daughter to not only the cobbler but also to each of the seven tradesmen who followed him as suitors, saying that none of them could support his daughter properly. The ninth suitor them came in. He turned out to be a well-to-do farmer. Such deep respect did the old father have for farming as a livelihood, that he would immediately agree to give the latest comer not one daughter only, but the whole nine of them! In the midst of the laughter evoked by the father's enthusiasm, the eight disappointed suitors would, as it were, proceed to abduct the daughters, only to be routed out of the wake-house by the angry father and his relatives. This game generally ended in a rough manner. It resembled a good deal a game played in England – not, however, at wakes – known by the name of Three Knights From Spain[40], and probably took its origin from it. Both the method of playing this wake-game and the verses used in it varied from one district to another. I do not know whether it was ever played at wakes where Irish was the normal language,

93

nor have I ever found Irish verses to suit it.

Other wake-games which were concerned with match-making and marriage include I Am a Poor Widow That Came from Athlone, The Silly Ould Man, Old Father Dowd, The White Cockade, and We are all a-marching to Quebec[41]. Henry Morris had described the last of these in *Béaloideas*,[42] and William Carleton gives an account of the others in *Traits and Stories of the Irish Peasantry*[43]. As all of the verses used were in the English language, it is unlikely that the games took hold in Irish-speaking areas.

Kissing; Frumso Framso; The Rope Game[44]

A number of wake-games involved kissing as a penalty, or otherwise. The most famous of these, Frumso Framso, has often been mentioned in episcopal pastoral letters. Its name varied: Carleton called it Frimsy Framsy[45]; the bishop of the diocese of Kildare and Leighlin, in a pastoral letter of 1748, termed it Fronsy fronsy[46]; and Most Rev. Dr. Thomas Bray, Archbishop of Cashel and Emly, in a letter to his flock in 1810 referred to it simply as Fraunces[47]. Its most general title throughout the country was, however, Frumso Framso. I would venture an opinion that these variations in nomenclature may be due to the fact that the name of the game was unintelligible to those who used it. I think that it may have been foreign in its origin – possibly having as its root the French word *français,* which simply means French. If this etymology is correct, it would signify that the game, with its name, originated in France. In the Irish-speaking areas, it was known as *Cleas an Stóilín* (The Stool Trick).

It was played as follows. A man sat on a chair or stool in the centre of the floor and asked a girl to come to kiss him. If the girl were unwilling to do so, two players, dressed in straw, would force her to obey. Having got the kiss, the man would leave his seat, and the girl took his place. The man whom she had just kissed would ask her: 'Frimsy, framsy, what's your fancy?'. She would then name some fellow, who would come either willingly or reluctantly to give her a kiss. So the game went on until the company tired of it.

As played in Irish-speaking areas, it differed slightly. A man who acted as leader in charge of the game would ask the man who was seated on the chair: 'What do you want for your dance?' His reply, in Irish, would be: 'A nice girl to be talking to.' 'Name her,' the leader would order. The girl who was named would then come willingly to kiss him, or else was forced to do so.

There is ample evidence that the clergy looked with disfavour on this game. Bishops often condemned it, as has been said, and a guide-book for the clergy concerning the hearing of Confessions, compiled by an Irish priest about 1743, has this to say with regard to sins against the Sixth Commandment:

'Did you promote any kind of Plays unbecoming those of a different sex? How often did you promote such Plays and Diversions, and how many persons did you engage in it at every time? Among these Plays you may reckon Frumsy Framsy used at weakes (*sic*) by the vulgar young People, the cause of a multitude of Sins. These Games and Plays are Hellish Artifices, which the Devil makes use of to convey without scruple unchaste Love and thoughts into the heart, because many of them are looked upon in the world as so many innocent recreations, but in truth most dangerous and malignant, and therefore absolutely to be forbidden[48].'

The Cure for a Sore Head

A man stood out on the floor, complaining of great pain in his head. Somebody in the audience would ask him what cure he suggested; the sick man would reply that nothing would cure him except that a certain fellow would kiss a certain girl. Now, the pair might be chosen with a mischievous purpose: the fellow might happen to be very shy, the girl also, or else she might be uncomely.

Still the cure had to be made effective, so the fellow was forced to kiss the girl. She too might mischievously complain that he had not kissed her properly, so he would be forced to kiss her again. The sick man would continue to complain, so he would name some other fellow and girl, for the kissing, and so the game went on.

Prey Boys; Jack Dowdall; The Horse Fair; Kiss in the Ring[49]

These names from different districts all referred to the same game. A girl took her seat on a stool in the centre of the kitchen. A number of young men would run into the kitchen, one by one, from outside, each reciting some verse at the same time. Each would then, in turn, leap-frog over the back of a man who was stooped down between him and the girl, and kiss her, whether she was willing or not. The game was also played as follows: a man sat on a stool in the middle of the floor, while a number of girls dances around him in a circle. When the man named one of them, she would have to go to kiss him.

Imitation of the Sacraments[50]

Marrying was a very common feature of wake-games[51]. As described in *Béaloideas*[52], it was played as follows: the game-leader would ask a man who sat on a chair in the middle of the floor what he wanted.

'A wife who would drink beer,
Who would be amusing,
And who would be punctual,'

was the reply. Some girl was then chosen from the audience, and she would have to go to the man on the chair. A second man, followed by others, then took turns on the chair, and wives were chosen for them in the same way. They were then married to one another.

William Carleton has given a description of this type of marriage-imitation, as played at wakes in South Tyrone between 1800 and 1815[53]. A male player would don an old black coat and wear on his head a wig or similar covering to simulate long hair. He was to act the part of the priest. He would start off by sending all the young fellows out of the wake-house and closing the door. He then got the girls to sit side by side within. After asking one of them what man she wished to marry, he would go out to bring him in. The priest, so-called, would then get the fellow and the girl to stand side by side on the floor, and, to the accompaniment of some Latin gibberish, he would proceed to marry them, as it were. The newly-married man would then sit down, his wife on his knee, and the 'priest' would kiss her. So the game continued until all the couples were 'married'.

A game of the same kind was named Leaping the Besom in other areas. A young fellow stood on the floor, with a ring or something of that kind in his hand. A girl whom he would name would then have to leap across a broom towards him; he would then place the ring on her finger, and they were 'married'.

The Marrying was played in the following manner in some districts: one man acted as the priest, and he would 'marry' a girl to the first man who came in from outside. A well-known story, associated with this game, tells how, as the girl was on the point of being 'married' to the man who had come in, she glanced down and saw that he had hooves instead of human feet — he was, in other words, the Devil!

It goes without saying that the clergy actively opposed marriage travesties of this kind.

A story is also told of what happened when this game was being played in a wake-house during Penal Times (roughly, the eighteenth century). A great many priests were 'on the run' at that time and went about secretly, clad in non-clerical garb. Such a priest came to a house at nightfall one evening and asked for shelter until morning. The only person in the house was a young woman, who welcomed him and gave him something to eat. As they chatted, he enquired whether she lived alone there. No, she told him; she lived there with her parents, but they had gone to a wake in a neighbouring house. The priest asked her why she had not gone also for company's sake, and she explained her position to him. She was in love with a young man of the parish, she said, but her love was not returned. At the wake, the marrying-game would be played and, as everybody knew the position, she would be mischievously chosen to 'marry' the man she loved, and this would cause her further heartbreak. The priest asked her to accompany him to the wake and, when the marrying-game was about to begin, he spoke to the leader of the game. Nobody recognised him as a priest. He asked if he might be allowed to show them how the game was played in his own district, far away, and, of course, they were eager to see this. The girl had already pointed out to the priest the man she loved, and they were the first pair he called on to come out to be married. When he had finished the game, he pulled open his coat and showed the people his clerical collar, telling the young man that he was as properly married as if the ceremony had taken place in church.

It is probable that this is just a story. Still, old people say that they often heard priests, who condemned this game, say from the pulpit that marriages performed as games at wakes were as binding as those in a church. This again is probably not true, as such 'marryings' were, be they right or wrong in the eyes of the clergy, performed only by way of amusement. It is well-known, however, that the clergy in many dioceses forbade girls, who were not close relatives of the deceased, to attend wakes in certain areas.

Hearing Confessions[54]

This was another travesty of a sacrament which formed the basis for a wake-game long ago. Some fellow would throw a red ribbon or a straw-rope around his neck, and sit in a corner to 'hear confessions', as would a priest or bishop. The rest of the company looked on as the 'penitent' confessed his sins. They would not hear his mumbled words, but whether the so-called sins were grave or not, the 'priest' pretended to be horrified by them and imposed a very severe penance on the 'sinner'. As this penance had to be performed in the wake-house, the audience had much occasion for laughter, owing to the ridiculous and embarrassing nature of most of the penances.

NOTES

1. Lady Wilde, *Anct. Leg.*, 120–121; Wood-Martin, *Elder Faiths*, I, 315.
2. Hartmann, *Totenkult*, 113.
3. *Anthol. Hib.*, 12/1794, 439; Hartmann, *Totenkult*, 113.
4. Wood-Martin, *Hist. of Sligo*, 348; Lady Wilde, *Anct. Leg.*, 122; Wood-Martin, *Elder Faiths*, I, 315; Hartmann, *Totenkult*, 117.
5. *Jour. Kilk. Arch. Soc.*, II, 334.
6. *Béaloideas*, VIII, 126, 137.
7. *op. cit.*, 334.
8. Gomme, *Trad. Games*, I, 120; cf. *ib.*, 346.
9. Hartmann, *Totenkult*, 116.
10. Gomme, *Trad. Games*, I, 120.
11. Gomme, *Trad. Games*, I, 120; Hartmann, *Totenkult*, 116.
12. *Béaloideas*, VIII, 138; Gomme, *Trad. Games*, I, 390; *ib.*, II, 83, 428; Brand, *Pop. Antiq.*, II, 250; Sutton-Smith, *op. cit.*, 147.
13. Gomme, *Trad. Games*, I, 390; do. II, 428.
14. Brand, *Pop. Antiq.*, II, 246; Gomme, *Trad. Games*, I, 108.
15. Gomme, *Trad. Games*, I, 120.
16. Wood-Martin, *Elder Faiths*, I, 318; Hartmann, *Totenkult*, 114.
17. *Béaloideas*, V, 232.
18. *Béaloideas*, V, 229.
19. *The Bell*, III, 313; see p. 70 of this book.
20. See page 76.
21. *Béaloideas*, V, 231; Gomme, *Trad. Games*, II, 16.
22. Hartmann, *Totenkult*, 117.
23. Gomme, *Trad. Games*, II, 404; Sutton-Smith, *op. cit.*, 108; Hartmann, *Totenkult*, 117.

24. Wood-Martin, *Elder Faiths*, I, 318; Gomme, *Trad. Games*, II, 189; *Béaloideas*, V, 229, 232.

25. *Béaloideas*, XII, 188–190; Strutt, *op. cit.*, 238–9.

26. *Anthol. Hib.*, 12/1794, 439; *Béaloideas*, VIII, 121.

27. *Ireland's Own*, LXV, 212; *ib.*, 13/2/1937, 20.

28. *Béaloideas*, X, 244–5.

29. Dineley, *Observations*, 34 (note by D. Kelly); Walter, *The Fascination of Ireland*, 99.

30. Hartmann, *Totenkult*, 116.

31. *Ar Aghaidh*, 12/1936, 5; Gomme, *Trad. Games*, I, 40, 227; Hartmann, *Totenkult*, 114.

32. Strutt, *op. cit.*, 342.

33. *Ireland's Own*, 13/2/1937, 20.

34. Ó Ruadháin, *op. cit.*, 120; Wood-Martin, *Hist. of Sligo*, 348; Gomme, *Trad. Games*, I, 121; Hartmann, *Totenkult*, 114.

35. *Folk-Lore*, V, 191.

36. Carleton, *Traits and Stories*, I, 105–6; Farewell, *Ir. Hudibras*, 34; *Hwbch. des d. Abergl.*, V, 1110; Hartmann, *Totenkult*, 117.

37. Edgeworth, *Castle Rackrent*, 214.

38. *Béaloideas*, VIII, 131–2; Gomme, *Trad. Games*, I, 315; do. II, 208, 257.

39. *Béaloideas*, II, 394–5; Wood-Martin, *Hist. of Sligo*, 348; *Folk-Lore*, V, 190; Gomme, *Trad. Games*, I, 206, 287.

40. Gomme, *Trad. Games*, II, 455.

41. Kennedy, *Boro*, 66; Wood-Martin, *Hist. of Sligo*, 348; *Dub. Univ. Mag.*, 8/1862, 153; Gomme, *Trad. Games*, I, 206, 351–2; *ib.*, II, 62, 63, 197, 199, 381, 451; Ó Ruadháin, *op. cit.*, 122; *Folk-Lore*, V, 191; Carleton, *Traits and Stories*, I, 111–2.

42. *Béaloideas*, VIII, 131.

43. *op. cit.*, 111–2.

44. *Béaloideas*, VIII, 139; Lady Wilde, *Anct. Cures*, 127; Wood-Martin, *Elder Faiths*, I, 318; Carbery, *The Farm by Lough Gur*, 169; Gomme, *Trad. Games*, I, 87, 145; Dineley, *Observations*, 34–L (notes by John O'Donovan).

45. Carleton, *Traits and Stories*, I, 107.

46. See page 149.

47. See page 151.

48. Marley, *The Good Confessor*, 165.

49. Wood-Martin, *Elder Faiths*, I, 318; do. II, 129–30; Wood-

Martin, *Hist. of Sligo*, 348; Carbery, *The Farm by Lough Gur*, 169; Lady Wilde, *Anct. Cures*, 130; *Béaloideas*, VIII, 127; Gomme, *Trad. Games*, I, 305.

50. Hartmann, *Totenkult*, 113.
51. Lady Wilde, *Anct. Cures*, 131, 133; *Anthol. Hib.*, 12/1794, 439; Murphy, *Slieve Gullion*, 73–4; Wood-Martin, *Hist. of Sligo*, 348; Carbery, *The Farm by Lough Gur*, 169; Anon., *The Irishman at Home*, 210–1, *Ireland Illustrated* (1844), 197–200; *Jour. Kilk. Arch. Soc.*, II, 334; G. J., *Original Legends*, 85–; Hartmann, *Totenkult*, 117.
52. *Béaloideas*, V, 230; *ib.*, X, 285.
53. Carleton, *Traits and Stories*, I, 109–110.
54. G. J., *Original Legends*, 86.

VI

CATCH GAMES

This type of game, whether played as a parlour-game or at wakes, had as its object the testing of the alertness and quick response of the players. It differed from the booby-trap, in that it had not the sole intention of making a fool out of somebody. In all catch-games, the quick-witted player was safe from punishment for being caught napping; his slower fellow-players were the sufferers.

The leader in these games tried to catch out those players who could not speak or act as quickly as was necessary. If, for example, he ordered the players to either perform a certain act, or its opposite, they had to obey him immediately or suffer the consequences. Sometimes he would endeavour to get them to say a word which the game forbade. Some players were always the victims when the orders came too quickly for them to respond, and they had no time to think about what they were supposed to do or say. Here follow some examples of these catch-games, many of which resembled imitative games.

The Tailors; Making the Breeches; Sewing the Big Coat[1]
The player who acted as master-tailor in this game stood in the centre of a circle of apprentices, who were seated on the floor. In some forms of the game, the apprentices were replaced by journeymen tailors who had been hired by the master to work for him. The master would start off the game by questioning each of them about his former employer, and had many sarcastic remarks to make about each in turn. This was intended to make the audience laugh, and it generally succeeded in its purpose. If they were journeymen, he would then make a bargain with them about their wages, on condition that they worked to his satisfaction.

102

Each player held in his hands some small piece of cloth, at which he worked with a stick, as needle; or else the whole group sat around a shawl or sheet, which was spread out on the floor, all busily pretending to sew its edges. In the centre of the shawl or sheet would lie a sod of turf or a small turnip – this was supposed to be a ball of thread, from which each of them occasionally took his share.

'Thread your needles, men!' the master would shout, and the tailors proceeded to carry out the order. 'Stretch out the material!' would be the next command; all would do as they were told. 'The servant and the master are all one,' the master would then remark, hinting, that, whatever he did himself, they also had to do. He would then throw off his coat; they all did the same, anyone who refused, or who was slow in obeying, being beaten by the master with a stick or strap. He went on giving similar orders in the same words, divesting himself of some garment each time; the helpers had to follow suit, or else be punished. They had to keep a sharp eye on the master all the while, for sometimes, when he had some garment half-off himself, he would suddenly change his mind and keep it on. If the master-tailor happened to be rather devoid of shame, the divesting of garments would go beyond proper bounds. Apart from this, it was a very amusing game, which the audience much enjoyed.

The game over, the master would set about paying the wages. This consisted in hoisting each of the helpers on to a man's back and giving him a blow of a stick or strap for each shilling which he might have earned!

The Dummy Band

Ten or twelve players sat in a circle on the floor, the conductor of the band standing in the centre. He assigned some musical instrument to each – a violin, a drum, a flute, and so on. He would then begin to conduct them as they played, each simulating his own part in the game. The conductor did not play at all; he merely held in his hand a small wand which he waved about. Suddenly, ceasing to conduct, he would start to imitate the actions of one of the band, or of more who might all have the one instrument, as it were. If this player or his fellows did not rise up immediately, the conductor would impose some suitable penalty.

The Polony Man

The Irish folklore journal, *Béaloideas*[2], has a reference to this game as having been played at a wake in Dublin City in 1939. Like the foregoing, it was based on music. The leader of the band pretended to play a particular musical instrument, and each of the other players had to imitate him. After a while, the leader would say:

> I'm the wee Polony man,
> The ratterin' tatterin' Tory man;
> I'll play all the tunes I can
> To catch the wee Polony man.

As soon as he had said this, he immediately began to simulate the playing of a different instrument. The others had to change over as quickly as the leader did; those who were slow in doing so were punished.

The game was played in a different manner in other areas. At first the players would pretend to be playing different instruments. Then the leader would say:

> I'm the wee Polony man,
> So do all you can
> To catch the wee Polony man.

As soon as he had said the last word, he would change over from whatever instrument he had hitherto played and use, as it were, a different one. If the leader changed, for example, from the flute to the fiddle, the player who had been using the fiddle until then was immediately expected to start on the flute, or else suffer a penalty. All the players had to keep a sharp eye on the leader to see which instrument he chose for himself each time after repeating the verse.

The Rule of Contrariness[3]

Seven or eight players sat in a circle on the wake-house floor, each taking a hold on a piece of cloth which was spread over their feet. The leader would then announce: 'Ye must do the opposite of whatever I order; if I tell you to pull, you must let go your hold; if I tell you to let go, you must pull.' He would then issue his orders so quickly that many players would be caught napping in doing the reverse, and a penalty was imposed on them.

Mr. Doodle

According to an account published in *Béaloideas*[4], this wake-game was played in North Dublin. All of the players, with the exception of the leader, sat on chairs in a semi-circle. The leader faced them. 'One hammer a-going for Mrs. Doodle!' he would order, at which each player, while repeating the same words, had to strike his own knee with his fist. The number of hammers was ordered into action by the leader until each player used six simultaneously: two fists against his knees, two feet against the floor, the head bobbing up and down, and the tongue moving in and out. It was difficult to keep all these 'hammers' going at the same time, but it was made harder still by the constant sudden changes in the number of hammers to be used, say, going from the whole six down to the correct three and so on. Each player had to remember, if he could, the order in which the 'hammers' came into use; if he could not, or if he was slow in changing, he was punished by the leader.

The leader also often introduced Mr. Doodle into the words to further confuse the players. At the mention of his name, the players had to stop all movement – not an easy thing to do, owing to the quick tempo of the game.

All Birds Fly

This wake-game is also mentioned in *Béaloideas*[5], the Irish folklore journal. A number of players sat in a semicircle, hands resting on their knees. In front of them stood the leader; his assistant walked around at the back of the players. If the leader named some bird by saying, for example, 'Crows fly,' each player was supposed to simulate the flight of a crow by flapping his hands. In the midst of this, he would name another bird, and the flapping continued. But suddenly, he might shout 'Cats fly' or 'Cows fly,' and all hands had to remain still. Any player who was not alert enough to obey the change was slapped with a strap by the leader.

Ducks Swim

This wake-game slightly resembled the previous one, except that the players had no actions to perform. They merely had to repeat the words of the leader, such as 'Ducks swim' or 'Crows fly' – two statements of truth. But if he said something which was untrue, such as 'Horses fly', each player had to remain silent. So quickly would the leader change his words, that players who were not very alert were easily caught out and had to suffer a penalty.

Horns; The Painter[6]

William Carleton has described this wake-game. A number of players sat in a circle on the floor, while the leader sat on a chair or stool in the centre, holding a vessel which contained soot or shoe-polish. He might say something like 'Horns, horns, goat-horns', at the same time using two fingers to indicate that he had horns on his forehead. The rest acted similarly. The leader spoke very quickly, changing suddenly, say, from goats to horses or pigs; any player who indicated horns for these animals was to suffer a penalty, such as a blow of a strap.

Other catch-games brought a penalty on those players who, for example, could not quickly, or at all, supply a suitable answer to the leader's question. Examples follow.

The Straw Trick; The Uses of Straw

A large number of players sat down on the floor, while their leader stood in the centre. He would begin by asking one player a question such as 'What might straw be used for?' That player would give a reply such as 'To feed cattle', another would say 'To thatch a house', or 'as a bed', and so on. By the time the leader had reached, say, the twentieth player, who was not allowed to repeat any earlier answer, he was often unable to name a further use for straw. All the others would laugh as he racked his brains for a suitable answer; if he failed, he was slapped with a strap.

The Sick Soldier; What Would You Give a Sick Soldier?

Again, the players sat in a circle, the leader in the centre. He would ask each in turn what he would give to a sick soldier. One might mention milk, a second tea, a third some kind of medicine, and so on. These were all fairly suitable and normal on such an occasion. But if a player, who was hard put to remember something new as a prescription, said, for example, potatoes or a blanket (which could not be eaten), or if he failed altogether to name anything, he was punished with a strap.

The Minister's Cat[7]

The leader in this game would say 'The minister has a black cat' or something like that, and each player in turn had to repeat this but insert some other adjective beginning with the letter 'b', as 'black' did. He might say 'The minister has a big cat' (or a brown, bad, bald etc. cat), but, if he could not remember some suitable adjective beginning with the prescribed letter, he was to suffer a penalty. The same procedure was followed in the Irish language (*dubh, donn, dána, dathúil,* and so on, being called for). Any letter of the alphabet in turn might be in use.

The foregoing was also a popular parlour-game; in New Zealand, it was known as Constantinople[8].

The purpose of still other catch-games at wakes was to get some players to say forbidden words. I have no information as to whether they were played in the Irish language. The forbidden words were Aye (I), Yes and No. Some examples of this type are given below.

Selling the Plough

The leader would, as it were, distribute parts of a plough among his fellow-players, giving one the coulter, a second the sock, and so on. He would then ask each in turn a number of questions, trying to trap him into using one of the forbidden words: Aye (or I, which had the same sound), Yes and No[9]. If he spoke of himself as 'I', he would be punished with a strap; similarly, if he used the word 'know', which resembled 'no' in sound. It was difficult to escape being trapped, so quickly did the questions come from the leader. If the leader failed to catch any of them napping, somebody else took over in his stead, until the game ended.

Buying the Fish, a somewhat similar game, was, we are told, played in North Dublin at wakes[10]. The account we have of it is not very clear, and does not relate to the title of the game given by the informant. The leader held a button between his closed palms and went about from one player to another, each of whom held his palms together. He would slip the button secretly in this way to one player. The leader would pretend that the button was a coin, and would enquire who had the money. Whoever had it admitted it, and he would then be questioned by the leader, as in the previous game, trying to trap him into saying Aye (I), Yes or No (Know). If he did so, he was punished.

Díol an Éisc (Selling the Fish) was another catch-game. The leader would give some kind of fish to each player to sell: herrings, as it were, to one, mackerel to a second, cod to a third, plaice to a fourth, and so on. He would then start to question each rapidly about the kind of fish he had to sell; those who might fail to reply quickly or correctly would be slapped or have soot rubbed to their faces.

Selling the Turf

Some twenty players could take part in this game, if the floor were big enough for all to sit on. The leader would announce that he had turf for sale. 'How much will you pay me for a load of it?' he would ask a player. 'Ten shillings,' he might reply. 'That's all you'll offer?' the leader would say, feigning surprise. 'It is worth double that money'. He would suddenly turn to some player at the other side of the circle, saying 'Will you give me more for it?'. If that player were unlucky enough not to have been listening carefully, he might offer, say eight shillings, even less than what the leader had already refused. As he was not supposed, by the rules of the game, to offer a smaller price than that already tendered, he would get a lively whack of a stick from the leader. All players had to keep their ears cocked in order to be ready for a sudden question from the leader, when least expected.

Other wake-games were intended to catch out players who might be slow in obeying the order of the leader. All Hammers (Sledges) on the Block[11], played only by English speakers, so far as I know, was an example. The leader gave each player a nickname: Ould MacShane, Young MacShane, Ould MacTaine, Young MacTaine, Hugasoo, Hugasoddy, Pick the Pot, Lick the Pan, and so on. From six to eight players might take part. The leader sat on a chair. One of the other players was then chosen by lot to go on his knees in front of the leader and place his head between the leader's knees. The other players stood in line behind the kneeling man. The leader might then shout: 'Hit him, Ould MacTaine!' at which the player so named would have to rush forward and strike the kneeling player with his fist on the back. So closely did some of the nicknames resemble one another, and so quickly did the leader give his orders, that the players might become confused. Any player who did not immediately obey the leader's order had to go down on his knees instead of the kneeling man. When the kneeler had finally been thumped on the back by each of the players, the leader would give the order: 'Single sledges on first!' Each of the players was then supposed to rush forward immediately and hit the kneeler on the back with a single fist; anyone who did not do this properly or who was slow in action had to take the place of the kneeler. The next order, which came even more suddenly, would be 'Double sledges on the block!' and all the players had to run forward and strike the kneeler on the back with both fists. If any one player had to kneel for a long time in this game, his back would be quite sore from the punching of the fists.

The Grass of the Goat

Eight men or so would sit in a circle on the floor, their shins bared. In the centre between them lay a sod of turf. Each player had been given a number by the leader, who held a wisp of straw across his mouth, which he tugged at while simulating the 'Meg-eg-eg' of a goat with his voice. He would suddenly shout out 'Meg-eg-eg Three!', and the player who had that number would immediately have to strike the sod of turf with a stick he held in his hand. If he failed to do so, he himself was struck with a stick on his bare shins by the leader. There would be many red shins in the kitchen by the time that game had come to a close!

All Round Your Daddy

Henry Morris has left a description[12] of the way in which this wake-game was played in Co. Monaghan. The leader played the part of Daddy, and the others stood around him in a circle. As he sang a song

We'll dance it in, we'll dance it out,
We'll dance it merrily round-about,

the other players danced in and out around him. He would suddenly change from the song to give the order: 'All round your Daddy, and the last man marked!' Whoever was slowest in obeying would have soot rubbed to his face as punishment. The leader would continue to sing, and they to dance, until he might suddenly give them the order to go on their knees or stand on their heads, for example. As it was impossible to anticipate these sudden orders many were caught off guard and ended up with blackened faces.

The Man and Woman of the House[13]

Ten or twelve players stood in a circle on the floor. Two others, representing the man and woman of the house, stood in the centre, the woman holding a vessel which contained a mixture of soot and butter. Each of the other players would have a nickname in the game: Jug, Mug, Can, Dish, Spoon, Knife, and so on. The man in the centre would suddenly twist himself and his wife about, saying, 'I turn *Bean an Tí*, I turn *Fear an Tí*. Who turns Dish?' As soon as he said this, the player named Dish had to turn himself about, or else his face would be smeared with the butter and soot. As the game was played with speed, many players ended up with blackened faces.

Players who were slow in replying to questions might be trapped in other wake-games. Examples of these were The Priest of the Parish, which was also known as My Man Jack and The Rates of the Market in other areas[14]. One player would don a hat or cap, pretending to be the parish priest. He would then give nicknames to the other players: Jack (his own servant), Black Cap, Red Cap, Plum Pudding, and so on. Taking off his headgear, the priest would say: 'The priest of the parish has lost his considering cap; some say this and some say that, but I say 'My Man Jack'.

Jack: 'Is it me, sir?'
Priest: 'Yes, you, sir'.
Jack: 'You lie, sir'.
Priest: 'Who then, sir?'

Jack would then name Black Cap or some other player. If the player named did not say immediately 'Is it me, sir?' he would be slapped.

Another method of playing this game was: the leader, holding a button or some other small object between his palms, would go from one player to another in turn, pretending to give it to each but giving it only to one. The questions and answers already quoted then went on; when the player who had the button was mentioned, he took over as leader[15].

People who were slow to answer questions would also be the targets in another catch-game, What's That Man's Name?[16] The leader stood in the centre of a ring of players on the floor, each of whom had been given a nickname, such as Ay Nib, Hay Nib, Harry McCauley, Jolly Neighbour, and so on. The leader would repeat each of the nicknames a second time. He would then suddenly point at some player and ask another player what the nickname of the other was. As it was difficult to remember the nicknames of all, many players failed to answer correctly and were slapped. Where this game was played by Irish speakers, the nicknames might be *Gibide Cabhsach, Cabhsach Crú, Crú Artúir, Artúr Crú, Gillín Gile, Fear Farcalán, Fear Callánach, Mac Uí Lorcáin*, and so on. Whoever forgot a name had soot rubbed to his face.

Another catch-game, which was mainly based on buying and selling, was known in different districts by such names as *Díol an Choirce* (Selling the Oats, or Straw), The Rates in the Market, Spy the Market, Selling the Corn or Barley, and Bird Loss[17]. The players sat in a circle on the floor, while their leader stood in the centre. The pretence was that grain was up for sale, and the leader gave various prices to be remembered by individual players: 2d., 4d., 6d., and so on. The leader would recite the following rhyme:

> Bun Glas was a man of honour and fame,
> And he earned his bread by this innocent game;
> If you don't remember what you are told,
> A beating you'll get when you are so bold!

The moment he had said the concluding word, he would suddenly ask one player what price had been given to another. If this player failed to answer correctly, he was either beaten with a strap or else struck with a dirty cloth.

The game was played as follows in some areas. When a price had been given to each player to remember, the leader would suddenly call out some price, and the player who had it was supposed to call it out aloud two or three times, or else suffer a penalty.

Ridirí; Knights

Béaloideas[18] has a description of the way in which this game was played at wakes in Co. Galway. Again, the players sat in a circle on the floor; the leader stood in the centre. He gave each player a title, such as First Knight, Second Knight, and so on. He would then address them, saying: 'Hail, O Knights!' Each player had to reply to this salute according to his rank; for example, the Fifth Knight would have to say 'Hail!' five times, and so on. Any player who failed to reply correctly, or who replied out of his turn, when he should remain silent, would be hoisted on to the back of another player and beaten with a strap, the leader saying *'Haliútar'* at the first blow, *'Fá méatar'* at the second, *'Bád éinne'* at the third, and *'Gabh anuas* (Get down)' at the fourth.

Selling the Knife, The Razor, or The Scissors

In this game, the players sat in pairs in a circle, while the leader stood in the centre. He would pretend that he had a razor (or knife or scissors) to sell; in the case of a razor, he would praise it highly – it was of the best of

113

steel, it would shave the whole world; it would last for ever; it was cheap at any price, and so on. He would suddenly ask some player if he wished to buy it. According to the rules of the game, this player might not answer himself; the reply had to come from the player who was his companion in the circle. The companion might say that the other had no need for a razor and, even if he had, the one which was on sale was a poor bargain. The game went on thus, with quick repartee and sarcasm on both sides, until the leader went on to try to sell the razor, as it were, to the next pair. The whole purpose of the leader was to catch somebody napping; as already stated, one of each pair had to remain silent while his companion replied to the leader and argued with him about the merits of the razor. If either of the pair failed in his part, he was beaten with a strap. The game continued thus until each pair had been tried out.

The Two-tailed Cat

This again was a trap-game. Both men and women might take part, standing beside one another in line, while the leader stood in front of them. He would hold in his hand a straw-rope, twisted to resemble a cat, and would first pass it on to the player at the head of the line. 'Here's a two-tailed cat for you,' he would say: 'Two tails?' this player would query, as he (she) examined the 'cat'. 'Yes', the leader would reply. The first player would then pass it to the next person and the same conversation would take place. The second player would be caught out if he (she) asked the first player had the cat really two tails; the question might only be addressed to the leader in each case. Any player who forgot this rule would either be beaten with a strap or have his face smeared with soot. When the end of the line had been reached by the 'cat', it would be passed back to the leader to start once more, the 'cat' now being supposed to have three tails. When the game was played at a fast tempo, as it usually was, players were easily caught out.

1. *Béaloideas*, III, 417; *ib.*, XIX, 182; Rev. J. Hall, *Tour*, I, 323; *Little, Malachi Horan*, 75.
2. *Béaloideas*, XI, 191; Gomme, *Trad. Games*, I, 129.
3. Gomme, *Trad. Games*, II, 383; Sutton-Smith, *op. cit.*, 115.
4. *Béaloideas*, XIX, 183.
5. *Béaloideas*, VIII, 139; *ib.*, X, 286.
6. Carleton, *Traits and Stories*, I, 112; Gomme, *Trad. Games*, I, 228.
7. Gomme, *Trad. Games*, I, 388.
8. Sutton-Smith, *op. cit.*, 109.
9. *Béaloideas*, XIX, 182; Gomme, *Trad. Games*, I, 139; *ib.*, II, 24, 115.
10. *Béaloideas*, XIX, 181.
11. Gomme, *Trad. Games*, I, 119; Strutt, *op. cit.*, 494.
12. *Béaloideas*, VIII, 133.
13. *Béaloideas*, VIII, 133.
14. Carleton, *Traits and Stories*, I, 111; Murphy, *Slieve Gullion*, 75; *Béaloideas*, VIII, 139; *Ulst. Review*, I, 131; *Ireland's Own*, 29/8/1936, 21; *ib.*, 27/11/1954; 15; Gomme, *Trad. Games*, I, 79, 301; *ib.*, II, 79; Sutton-Smith, *op. cit.*, 110; Hartmann, *Totenkult*, 115.
15. See page 116.
16. *Dub. Univ. Mag.*, 8/1862, 156; Kennedy, *Boro*, 74.
17. *Béaloideas*, VIII, 135; *The Bell*, III, 313.
18. V, 230.

VII

GAMES OF HIDE, SEEK, AND
GUESSING

Many wake-games involved either the hiding of some object and the search for it, or else the search for some player who had hidden himself[1]. Or else, players had to guess what the hidden object was or where it was to be found. Blindfolding of the eyes was a necessary feature of many of these games.

The Button Game; Hide the Button; Who Has the Button?; Passing Around the Button or Ring, were different names for this form of amusement[2]. A large number of players, both men and women, might take part, either standing or sitting. The leader held between his palms a button, ring or some other small object. He passed around from one to one of the others, each of whom held his (her) own palms together as the leader did, and while he pretended to give the object to each and all, he really gave it only to one. The player who received it would show no sign of being the recipient. Each player would then be called upon to guess who had the object, and those who guessed incorrectly were beaten with a strap. In some areas, instead of being beaten, each of those who had missed had to give up to the leader some personal token (handkerchief, comb, knife etc.). When the leader had acquired these tokens, one player went down on his knees on the floor, with the hands covering his eyes. The leader would then pick out one of the tokens in his hand and say: 'I have a little thing here, and it is worth hundreds of pounds.' The kneeling player would ask: 'Is it silk or satin, or does it belong to a young girl?' If it did, the leader would reply: 'It is silk and satin, and belongs to a young girl.' The player had then to guess to whom it belonged. If he did so correctly, the owner of the token

116

had to suffer a penalty; if not, he had to suffer one himself, and continue to guess further. In some areas, if a player guessed correctly at the first attempt who had the button, he was promoted to be leader.

Guessing the Boxes

About ten players, men or women or both, sat on the bare floor, or else on ferns or straw which might be strewn on it. The leader of the game would have three or four small boxes in front of him on a table, one with, maybe, an egg in it, a second a pebble, a third a match or bead, and so on. The players were asked in turn to guess what was in the first box. If a man guessed correctly, he would be given a bit of tobacco to chew; a girl would get a bit of bread. Those who failed to guess correctly would be pursued around the kitchen, while being beaten on the shins with a stick, and would be forced to swallow a couple of eggs. The game continued with different penalties being imposed on those who failed, and often ended in fights as a result.

Blind Man's Buff[3]

This very popular type of parlour-game was also played at wakes and had several Irish names: *Folach Cruach, Dalla Púicín, Dallóg,* and *Cluiche na gCochall.* One player, who was blindfolded, had to make his way around the kitchen, trying to overtake and catch hold of one of those who were trying to escape him. A player who was caught would be punished by having his face smeared with soot or in some other way. As played in some areas, the blindfolded person had not only to catch somebody but also to name him; as those who were trying to escape usually exchanged garments, it was difficult to identify the person who was caught.

Hide the Robber[4]

Two players remained in the kitchen, while all others taking part had to remain outside until they were called upon to come in. They would then find only one of the other pair in the kitchen; the other had gone ahide somewhere, and each in turn had to guess where he was.

Hide the Linger

As stated earlier in this book, the linger was a strap or piece of rope used in wake-games for beating those who suffered a penalty. In the game named here, each player had to keep his eyes closed while the leader hid it somewhere in the house. Each had then to search for it, and the player who found it became leader.

An Luch Bheag; The Little Mouse[5]

This was in essence a search-game, and very rough it was, too. It began by two men, carrying sticks, entering the kitchen of the wake-house. One of them also carried in his hand a small *cadhrán* of turf, and this he would throw under the feet of those who were sitting in the wake-house. This bit of turf was the mouse, as it were, and the pair would begin to search under the feet of the seated people for it. Its main value to the two players was that it offered them an opportunity of handling anybody and everybody as roughly as they wished.

Hurry the Brogue[6]

This game was probably the most popular and most widely-spread wake-game of all. As a parlour-game it was known as Hunt the Slipper, but when played at wakes in almost every district in Ireland, it had very many names: *Thart an Bhróg; Bróg; Rata; Ridirí; Harra; Búta;* Shuffle the Brogue; Fox Harra; Brogue About; Bout; Hurra Burra; Hide the Gully; and Fool in the Middle. I should not be surprised to learn that there were even more names for it[7].

William Carleton called it Sitting Bróg, as played at wakes in Co. Tyrone[8]. A number of boys and girls would sit down in a circle on straw on the floor, and more straw would be scattered loosely over their legs. The leader stood in the centre, and his task was to guess which player had the *bróg* (shoe) in his possession at any particular moment of the game. At the start of the game, the shoe (or other object – it might be a piece of hard rope, a hat, a pipe, a cap, a stocking filled with sand, or anything at all) would be in the hands of some player, under the straw. The players would all shout simultaneously *'Thart a' bhróg! Thart! Thart!'* (Pass the shoe around! Pass it! Pass it!), and at the same time they all tossed the straw with their hands, as if each were passing the shoe to his (her) neighbour. If the shoe reached any player, he or she might keep it or pass it along under his (her) legs, while all the others acted similarly. It was very difficult for the leader in the centre to detect the person who had the shoe. He might wheel around suddenly to see if it might be in the possession of a player at his back; then when he was sure that he had spotted the right person, he might be struck from behind by the person who really had it. No matter how quickly he turned around again, the shoe would have vanished somewhere under the tossing straw. The players kept up their shouts of *'Thart a' bhróg!'* all the time until the shoe was finally located by the leader who had suffered many a blow during the game.

The locating of the shoe ended the first half of the game, which then continued as follows: the player in whose possession the shoe had been found had to undergo some penalty. This might be to have soot smeared on his (her) face, or else he had to stoop down from a sitting position; another player would sit beside him and thump him on the back with alternate fists, saying 'Hurly burly, thump on the back, how many horns do I hold up?'[9] (this would be something like *'Crungaide, crangaide'* etc., when played in Irish). As the second player said 'how many horns do I hold up?' he would lift up one or more of his fingers, or none, and the bent player had to guess how many 'horns' were sticking up. If he failed to do this, an even heavier penalty was imposed. Some object, such as a dish or plate or basin, would be placed on his bent back to the accompaniment of the words 'Heavy, heavy, what is on your back?' ('*Trom, trom, cad tá os do chionn?*' in Irish), and he had to guess what the object was. If he failed in this also, other objects in turn would be added to his load, until he finally succeeded in making the correct guess. Instead of this latter penalty, in some districts the person who was found in possession of the shoe had to take the place of the leader – no small penalty in itself.

The second half of the game just described, beginning with 'Heavy, heavy, what is on your back?', might be played as an independent game in its own right. For example, a number of men would sit on their haunches on the floor, one leg bent under the body, the other extended on the floor. Another player would stand in front of them, stick in hand, and recite a kind of doggerel verse in either Irish or English. The latter went as follows:

'Cheerily, Charlie, lambs locks, nine mice in a flock; out came Tod with his long rod and walloped them all from wall to wall: Allister dear, will you lend me your spear to write to the king for some of his gear; rock, reel, spinning-wheel, about the bonny wee row.'

As the leader said these words, he would tip the extended feet in turn with his stick, and the player whose foot was touched as the last word was said had to leave the game[10]. Thus it went on until finally only two players were left: the leader and one other. The latter had then to suffer a penalty of some kind, such as dipping his head into a bucket of water, or else he had to bend down and guess what objects were being placed on his back, as already described.

In some districts, Hurry the Brogue was known by the name of *Ridirí* (Knights). The start of the game was as already described, but when the shoe had been found in somebody's possession, the leader would ask the two strongest men at the wake to come on to the floor. One of them he would call First Knight, the other Second Knight. First Knight would hoist on to the back of Second Knight the player who had been caught with the shoe; the leader would then punish the unlucky player by striking him hard blows on the back, saying: 'One, fall, one'; 'Two, fall, two'; 'Three times, down'; 'Four, come down; '*Búirthín, áirthín*, do your duty and be mannerly'. Each of these phrases was said to the accompaniment of a heavy blow with a strap[11].

William Carleton has also mentioned a wake-game, called Weds or Forfeits, which he had seen played at a wake[12]. This game had other names in some areas: *Ag Gabháil Fhoinn* (Singing or Playing Music), Auctioning the Caps, The Song of the Hat, Raising the Pledges, and so on[13]. It was played as follows, with some minor local variations. Each player had to give up some personal token to the leader of the game: a knife, a pipe, a box of matches, a handkerchief or a garment of some kind. These were all thrown in a heap on the floor. The leader would then pick up one of them and enquire: 'Whose is this?' Whoever owned it would say so. The leader would then tell him what he must do: sing a song, play a tune, or some such task. If he did not fulfil the order, or was unable to get a substitute to perform on his behalf, the token which had belonged to him would be thrown into the fire.

This game was played in other ways also. When the tokens had been handed up to the leader by the players, somebody else was blindfolded and knelt, placing his face against the knees of the leader who would be seated on a stool or chair. The leader would then take one of the tokens in his hand and ask the blindfolded person what its owner would have to do. The owner would then have to obey, or else suffer a penalty.

The stooped or kneeling player was the person who had to undergo a penalty in this game, as played in certain districts. The leader would hold up one of the surrendered tokens and say to the blindfolded player: 'Fine, fine, super-fine; who is the owner of this?' If he did not guess correctly, the bandage was removed from his eyes, and a penalty was imposed: to eat a raw potato, for example, or drink a quart of water, or chew a piece of soap, or wash a girl's face or kneel and ask a certain girl to marry him. It was not hard to think of embarrassing penalties, and the game had to be stopped if they went beyond the bounds of decorum.

In other districts still, the game was known as *Cluiche na Sop* (The Wisps Game)[14]. The leader held in his hand a dozen stalks of straw; some were long, others short. Each player had to draw a stalk for himself; those who drew long ones escaped a penalty; but the others had to suffer in some way: kiss the ugliest girl present, or walk barefoot around the outside of the house nine times, or stand on his head for ten minutes or carry the heaviest man present around the house on his back.

NOTES

1. Henderson, *Notes*, 28–47; Gomme, *Trad. Games*, I, 211, 213–4.
2. *Béaloideas*, VIII, 139; *ib.*, XIX, 182; Murphy, *Slieve Gullion*, 77; *Ireland's Own*, 29/8/1936, 21; Little, *Malachi Horan*, 76; Sutton-Smith, *op. cit.*, 106; Gomme, *Trad. Games*, I, 96, 137, 327–8; *ib.*, II, 227, 408.
3. Wakefield, *Ireland*, II, 807; Croker, *Researches*, 170; Rev. J. Hall, *Tour*, I, 324; Rodenberg, *Pilgrimage*, 182; *Ireland's Own*, 16/7/1955, 7; Brand, *Pop. Antiq.*, II, 238; Hagberg, *op. cit.*, 241; Sutton-Smith, *op. cit.*, 105; Strutt, *op. cit.*, 499.
4. Henderson, *Notes*, 28–47; Gomme, *Trad. Games*, I, 211, 213–4.
5. Hartmann, *Totenkult*, 114.
6. *Béaloideas*, V, 229; *ib.*, VI, 126; *ib.*, VIII, 136; *ib.*, X, 285; *ib.*, XI, 175; *ib.*, XIX, 181; *Folk-Lore*, V, 191; *Ulst. Review*, I, 131; *Ar Aghaidh*, 12/1936, 5; *The Shamrock*, XXXI, 180; *An Claidheamh Soluis*, 19/4/1902, 105; *Ireland's Own*, 27/11/1954, 15; Lady Wilde, *Anct. Cures*, 129; Wood-Martin, *Elder Faiths*, I, 314–5; Carleton, *Traits and Stories*, I, 107; Wood-Martin, *Hist. of Sligo*, 348;

Carbery, *The Farm by Lough Gur*, 169; Wakefield, *Ireland*, II, 807; Croker, *Researches*, 170; Rev. J. Hall, *Tour*, I, 324; Brand, *Pop. Antiq.*, II, 250; Hagberg, *op. cit.*, 241; Sutton-Smith, *op. cit.*, 105; Gomme, *Trad. Games*, I, 121, 341; *ib.*, II, 36, 225, 241, 449, 454; Strutt, *op. cit.*, 494; Hartmann, *Totenkult*, 112.

7. Goldsmith, *Vicar of Wakefield* (1904), 62.

8. *op. cit.*, I, 107.

9. *Béaloideas*, XIII, 40–79; Gomme, *Trad. Games*, I, 37, 46, 346; Sutton-Smith, *op. cit.*, 139.

10. 'An Connachtach Bán', *Na Spiadóirí*, 27; *Ireland's Own*, LIII, 228; Gomme, *Trad. Games*, II, 449–450; cf. *Béaloideas*, X, 209 (as a parlour-game); Ó Fotharta, *Siamsa*, 16, 78, do.

11. Dunton (third letter: MacLysaght, *Irish Life in the Seventeenth Century*, 360–).

12. Carleton, *op. cit.*, I, 111.

13. *The Shamrock*, XXXI, 180; MacDonagh, *op. cit.*, 374; Wood-Martin, *Hist. of Sligo*, 348; Gomme, *Trad. Games*, I, 137–8; *ib.*, II, 326–7, 408–9, 429; Sutton-Smith, *op. cit.*, 108.

14. Gomme, *Trad. Games*, II, 205.

VIII

VARIOUS OTHER GAMES

There remain a few other wake-games still to be described, which do not easily fit into any of the foregoing categories.

The next three games were based on the attempts made by a player (in one case, by an animal) to break into or out of a circle of other players, who did all in their power to prevent him from doing so.

Muc (Torc) Isteach; Putting the Pig in the Sty (or to Bed); The Bull and the Cow[1].

This game was popular as a parlour-game in many countries. The players stood close together in a circle on the floor, their arms across one another's shoulders to keep the ring intact. In the centre sat a girl on some other player's knees. A single player (the Boar or Pig) stood outside the circle; his task was to break through the ring and kiss the girl. He had to try to make his way in between some player's legs, or else between the legs of two adjoining players; this was very difficult to do. If he succeeded in inserting his neck and head between some two legs, their owners would squeeze on them until he was almost choked, and he had to withdraw, if he were able. The players who formed the ring moved about and shouted noisily as they tried to protect the girl from the intruder, and it sometimes happened that a player or two would be hurt in the game. If the Boar finally succeeded in breaking through and kissing the girl, the player on whose knees she sat had to take his place.

Kick the Cobbler[2]

In this game, a player tried to break out through a surrounding circle of players. Those who formed the ring sat on the floor barefoot; in the centre stood a player, sometimes called the Cobbler, who had to escape through the ring. The seated players would lean backwards slightly and try to stop him by kicking him from all sides with their feet. If he did get through, the player who had allowed him to pass had to take his place.

Madra Beag; Little Dog

This game resembled the foregoing one, except that in it the escaper was a dog, not a person. Eight or so players sat on their haunches on the floor in the form of a circle. In the centre stood a man, with a dog; the smaller the dog, the better the chance it had of escaping, as it was hard to catch. 'Break out and they'll pay dearly!' the man would urge the dog, as he pushed him forward; the dog ran around the circle looking for an outlet, while the defenders shouted to each other: 'Keep it in! Keap it in!' So excited would the poor dog become that it would finally succeed in jumping across the ring or else find its way between two players. The player who had allowed it to escape had to suffer a penalty, such as turning nine somersaults on the floor. This is the only wake-game, apart from Cock-fighting, in which, so far as I know, an animal or bird was used.

Fox and Hounds[3]

This game, which was also popular outside of wakes, was based on escape and pursuit. A fairly large space was needed for it. The players stood in line, one behind another, all legs apart. At the head of the line stood a player to represent the fox; at the other end was the hound, as it were. The two tried to peer around the other players to catch sight of each other. When the hound started to chase the fox, he had to run in the same direction as the other; he was not allowed to suddenly turn around and run to meet him. The line of pursuit would be either around the standing players or else up or down between their legs. If the hound failed after three rounds to catch the fox, the latter was free to retire from the game, and the next player in line took his place. The hound had to keep up his role until he succeeded in catching some fox.

The Standing Tailors, described by Henry Morris, was a somewhat similar game, as played in Co. Monaghan[4]. The master-tailor stood on the floor, carrying a heavy strap, while his apprentices stood in line in front of him, one behind another, all facing towards the master. The master would start the game by pretending that the first apprentice in line had made a pair of breeches badly, had sewn on the buttons in the wrong places, and so on. The apprentice would not take the blame silently, and would counter with an accusation that the master himself had spoiled a suit which he had made for a certain man. Their tempers rose as they argued, until finally the master lost patience and pursued the apprentice around the line of players in an endeavour to catch him. As they both ran between the legs of the players, one of the latter might close his own legs and prevent his fellow-apprentice from escaping further. The master would then take hold of him and beat him well. So the game continued until they tired of it.

The Fox in the Hole[5]

This game also resembled the two foregoing ones, but it was rougher. As the player, who represented the fox, was being chased around the line of standing players and up and down between their legs, two players at the head of the line would pretend to help the fox[6] by dragging him out from the hole (legs), but while doing so, they made sure of smearing his face with a mixture of soot and sand, if they did not like him. Similarly, players in the line would crush and bruise with their knees both pursuer and pursued, if they happened to be unpopular for some reason.

The following wake-games have no similarity, one with another, or with any other games which have been described so far.

Choose Your Fancy

Some of the players would leave the wake-house, while others remained inside. The latter were given individual names by the leader: Whiskey, Stout, Beer, Wine, Tea, Butter-milk, and so on. The leader would then call upon one of those who were outside, and when he entered he would be asked what he would like to drink. If he happened to choose, say, beer, he would have to carry the person to whom that nickname had been given – heavy though he be – around the kitchen on his back. That was the drink he got! The game continued until each of those outside had been called in and given a 'drink'. A somewhat similar game was based on the colours of horses as nicknames.

The Clappy Dance

The 'dance' in this game was performed by the hands of two players who struck each other's palms, keeping time with either dance music which was being played for them or else lilting carried on by themselves. They sat on chairs facing each other, clapping their own knees and their opposite number's palms alternately, in time with the music. One of them would then change the pattern by striking his own right palm against the other's right palm; then the left against the left, and so on. It was a game which required expertness and practice as the movements were somewhat complicated.

Moods

Players sat in pairs on a stool, facing the leader who stood in front of them, strap in hand. He would order one pair to cry, a second pair to laugh, a third to remain as they were, and a fourth to grimace. It was not easy for the players to carry out their own assignments when they heard and saw what others were doing. All might quickly start to laugh! The leader slapped those who disobeyed his orders. After a while, the leader would transfer the duty from one pair to another all round, so that, for example, those who had been crying at first now had to laugh. This game gave much enjoyment to players and audience.

Polishing the Shoes

This game was rather like those earlier ones in which each player in turn had to perform a certain task. All, except the leader, sat in a circle on the floor. He would then call on one of them to come and polish his shoes. When this had been done, the leader would ask what the payment was. The man who had done the polishing, as it were, would say that he wanted someone in the ring to sing a song; if that player could not sing or refused to, he would be expelled from the kitchen with blows from the strap.

The Walls of Troy

Thomas Crofton Croker mentioned this wake-game in one of his books[7], published in 1824. He said that he had never seen it played outside of Ireland and expressed the opinion that it must be a very ancient game, so widespread was it in this country. He was unable, unfortunately, to give a satisfactory account of the way in which it was played.

Alice Bertha Gomme, in her account of traditional games in these islands[8], has mention of one called Troy Town or Troy Walls, which was popular in England and Wales, but I cannot say whether it was the same as that mentioned above by Croker.

Short Castle

Croker has also mentioned this as a wake-game played in the South of Ireland[9]. A square wooden board was used, on which lines were drawn from side to side, dividing it into four equal parts, as well as two diagonal lines. The four lines met and crossed one another in the centre of the square. Each of the two players who took part had three marbles or three shells. It is not easy, from Croker's description, to see clearly how the game was played, but it would seem that the winner was the player who succeeded in moving his marbles (or shells), one at a time, until they were all in a straight line. It reminds one somewhat of the well-known game called Noughts and Crosses.

NOTES

1. Wood-Martin, *Elder Faiths*, I, 315; *ib.*, II, 80, 129–130; Lady Wilde, *Anct. Legends*, 122–3; *Ireland's Own*, LXIII, 732; *Béaloideas*, VIII, 139; Hartmann, *Totenkult*, 114; Sutton-Smith, *op. cit.*, 146; Hagberg, *op. cit.*, 241.
2. Gomme, *Trad. Games*, I, 50, 142, 145.
3. Sutton-Smith, *op. cit.*, 145; Strutt, *op. cit.*, 487.
4. *Béaloideas*, VIII, 136.
5. cf. *Béaloideas*, VIII, 136.
6. Gomme, *Trad. Games*, II, 310.
7. *Researches*, 171.
8. Gomme, *Trad. Games*, II, 310.
9. Croker, *Researches*, 171.

IX

THE KEENING OF THE DEAD[1]

The expression of their sorrow by the relatives of someone who has died, especially if the loss is deeply felt, is a very natural human action. As already mentioned, however, people in many parts of Ireland traditionally refrained from keening the dead until they were fairly sure that the soul had really left the body. No tear was shed openly until the body had been laid out by some neighbourly women who had practice at this sad task. The lapse of time has been explained by the folk-belief that the Devil's dogs lay in wait for passing souls and might be roused from their sleep by the premature keening of the relatives. Once the body had been laid out for the wake, however, the danger would have passed, or so it was thought, and the keening might begin.

The immediate relatives then gathered around the corpse and wept and sobbed over it for a while. If the father were dead, the mourners would be his wife and any grown sons or daughters who were present. Young children would not take part; they were usually sent to some kind neighbour's house for the duration of the wake. While crying and sobbing in a broken-hearted way, the sad relatives would mention the name of the dead one and call upon him, sometimes asking why did he die. After a time, when the main paroxysm of grief had subsided, some sympathetic neighbours would draw the relatives back from the bedside and gently usher them out of the room.

If some absent member of the family or a close relative of the deceased arrived at the house during the wake, the members of the family would again assemble around the body to join with him in his grief. The women folk were much more demonstrative than the men and less restrained in their crying. Before the body was placed in the coffin at the close of the wake, the relatives would again gather together and mourn; they wept copiously too as the funeral left the house, and finally, in the graveyard as the clay was thrown on top of the coffin in the grave.

When the Irish language was spoken generally in former times, many people had the gift of poetry. This was shown in the numerous folk-songs and poems in Irish which have come down to us, though still more must have been lost altogether. We may expect, therefore, that many of the lamentations about the corpse at wakes and funerals were in the form of extempore poetry in Irish, and such was the norm. One of the relatives who possessed the gift would mournfully recite some verse in praise of the deceased, lamenting his death, and others would join in with sobs and additional words. Eugene O'Curry, in his Introduction to his monumental *Manners and Customs of the Ancient Irish*[2], has described such a scene: 'I once heard in West Muskerry, in the county of Cork, a dirge of this kind, excellent in point of both music and words, improvised over the body of a man who had been killed by a fall from a horse, by a young man, the brother of the deceased. He first recounted his genealogy, eulogised the spotless honour of his family, described in the tones of a sweet lullaby his childhood and boyhood, then changing the air suddenly, he spoke of his wrestling and hurling, his skill at ploughing, his horsemanship, his prowess at a fight in a fair, his wooing and marriage, and ended by suddenly bursting into a loud, piercing, but exquisitely beautiful wail, which was again and again taken up by the bystanders. Sometimes the panegyric on the deceased was begun by one and continued by another, and so on, as many as three or four taking part in the improvisation.'

Samples of these impromptu lamentations have been handed down to us orally; old people knew many of them by heart. Here is how a Kerry woman mourned her dead son at his wake:

Mo thaisce's mo ghamhain tu,
Mar bhuachaillín ceann-dubh,
Gur ghile liom thu ná an leamhnacht
'S ná uisce lae an tsamhraidh!

(My treasure and my love,
My little dark-headed boy,
Whom I thought whiter than new milk
Or than water on a summer day!)

An old man from the Decies gave me the following lament made by a widow over the body of her husband who had been a ploughman:

Éirigh suas id'_sheasamh,
A's gaibh do sheisreach capall!
Tóg fód chúig n-órdla ar treasnacht;
Féach ormsa, a thaisce,
'S gan tada 'gam mar thaca,
Ag dul ag baint ná ag gearradh!
Cé dhéanfaidh gnó an mharga?
Cé raghaidh go Cnoc an Aifrinn,
A's tusa sínte feasta? Och, ochón!

(Rise and stand up,
And tackle your ploughing-team!
Plough a five-inch furrow;
Look at me, my treasure,
With nobody to help me
When I go reaping or cutting!
Who will do my business at the market?
Who will go to the Hill of the Mass,
As you lie stretched from now on? Och, ochón!)

As I have mentioned poetic lamentations, I cannot pass silently over the thousands of elegies and dirges which form an important part of Irish poetry. These were not, as a rule, recited over the corpse, but were composed at some later stage. They may be termed literary compositions. One of the best-known is the Lament for Art

O'Leary[3], made by his wife, Dark Eileen O'Connell, when her husband was killed. Others of a similar kind are the dirges composed by five poets in a competition to mourn the tragic death of the Kerry chieftain, Mac Fineen Dubh, at Rathcahill, Co. Limerick, over one hundred years ago[4]. Still another, from which I quote two verses below, was the touching lament[5] composed by Patrick Hegarty, a Kerryman, living in Springfield, Mass., in August, 1905, when his little son died.

Ochón, a Dhoncha, mo mhíle cogarthach, fén bhfód so sínte
Fód an doichill 'na luí ar do cholainn bhig, mo loma-sceimhle!
Dá mbeadh an codla so i gcill na Dromad ort nó i n-uaigh san iarthar,
Mo bhrón do bhogfadh, cé gur mhór mo dhochar, 's ní bheinn id' dhiaidh air!

Is feoidhte caithte tá na blátha scaipeadh ar do leaba chaoil-se;
Ba bhreá iad tamall, ach thréig a dtaitneamh; níl snas ná brí ionnta.
Tá an bláth ba ghile liom dár fhás in ithir riamh, ná d'fhásfaidh choíche,
Ag dreó sa talamh, a's go deó ní thacfaidh, ag cur éirí croí orm!

(Ochón, my Donagh, my thousand loves, stretched under this sod –
This inhospitable sod which lies on your little breast, my bitter torture!
If you were thus asleep in Dromad churchyard or in some western grave,
My sorrow would soften, great though be my loss, and I would not grudge it!

Withered and spent are the blossoms which were laid
on your narrow bed;
Fine they were once, but they faded; now they have
neither colour nor life.
My own blossom, brighter than any that has ever
grown or will grow,
Rotting away in the earth, never again to return to
raise my heart!)

While it cannot be said that the poets who composed such literary laments were lacking in a deep feeling of sorrow still it must be remembered that, in most of them, the first intention of the poet was to express his thoughts in beautiful language, according to the traditional mode, rather than to show his deep personal loss. For the latter, we must look to the bedside laments composed by the near relatives.

In olden times, and in many parts of the world, the relatives of the dead person were not satisfied that their own keening properly filled the demands of the sad occasion. Thus there grew up a custom of hiring practised keeners to wail and cry over the dead. These keeners were paid for their simulation of sorrow. The Italian poet, Virgil, mentioned this practice as carried on among the Phoenicians:

Lamentis gemituque et foemino ululatu tecta fremunt.

(They shake the roof with their female crying and lamentation)[6].

Women keeners were much in vogue too at wakes and funerals throughout Europe and in Africa[7].

As regards the custom in Ireland, an account, by an anonymous traveller, of a Kildare wake in 1683 has the following to say: 'as soon as the bearers have taken up the body, they begin their shrill cries and hideous hootings... and if there be not enough to make out a good cry they hire the best and deepest mouthed in all the country and so they proceed towards the church; this now may be heard two miles or more. When they come at the church-yard on this occasion, (and at other times also) perhaps 5, 10 or 20 years after their husband, friend or relation has been buried, they repair to their graves, where they kneel over them, knocking and beating upon the grave and praising the party, repeating the former kindnesses have passed between them, intreating that they would attend and give ear to them, then in an odd tone sorrowing and lamenting their loss complain and tell them how they are misused and by whom injured and thereon pray their help to right them; and thus they continue commonly until some compassionating friend or neighbour come and lift them from the ground with expostulating language, so they return satisfied as having given an account to one that in time may redress their injuries, revenge or relieve them. The women are mostly inclined and observed to practise these things, and many the like a more anxious eye might discover amongst them[8].

James Farewell in *The Irish Hudibras*[9], a mock Aeneid about Ireland, which he published in 1689, has this to say about keening women:

They raise the cry, and so they fout him
Into a crate to howl about him;
Where, in one end, the parted brother
Was laid to rest, the cows in t' other
With all his followers and kin,
Who, far and near, come crowding in,
With hub-bub-boos, beside what cryers
For greater state his highnes (*sic*) hires.

W. King, in the *Art of Cookery*[10], published in 1776, says:

So at an Irish funeral appears
A train of drabs with mercenary tears;

Who, wringing of their hands with hideous moan,
Know not his name for whom they seem to groan,
While real grief with silent steps proceeds,
And love unfeigned with inward passion bleeds.

Mrs. S. C. Hall, an Englishwoman, who visited Ireland more than once in the company of her husband about the middle of the last century, gave an account of wake customs and was severely critical of the hiring of female keeners (*Ireland*, I, 221-231). These women received payment, from a crown to a pound, for their services. Mrs. Hall quotes the following lines of poetry concerning them:

They live upon the dead,
By letting out their persons by the hour
To mimic sorrow when the heart's not sad.

Eugene O'Curry stated that the usual number of hired keeners was at least four. 'One stood near the head of the bed or table on which the corpse was laid, one at the feet, who was charged with the care of the candles, and one or more at each side; the family and immediate friends of the deceased sat around near the table. The mourner at the head opened the dirge with the first note or part of the cry; she was followed by the one at the foot with a note or part of equal length, then the long or double part was sung by the two side mourners, after which the members of the family and friends of the deceased joined in the common chorus at the end of each stanza of the funeral ode or dirge, following as closely as they could the air or tune adopted by the professional mourners. Sometimes one or more, or even all the principal singers, were men.' O'Curry says further that a famous Kerry harper of the seventeenth century revived some remarkable laments for the dead, and that these were still current in his own day[11].

There is abundant evidence that foreign visitors to Ireland regarded the hiring of male or female keeners as a national disgrace[12]. So too did the Irish clergy, as will be seen later, who regarded such artificial sorrow and lamentation as abhorrent. Still, it was a traditional custom, and people continued to observe it down through the centuries. The more a dead person was mourned, even in such an unreal way, the better it was. Keening was an intrinsic part of both the wake and the funeral and, like so many other practices associated with death, was discontinued only with great reluctance.

Paid keeners received food and drink at wakes and funerals. Foreign travellers to Ireland have said that the pitch and quality of their simulated howlings noticeably increased after they had been given a large glass of strong whiskey! The people who hired and entertained them expected a good performance, the louder the better. A story is told of the dissatisfaction of a woman in West Kerry with the short lament of the keeners over her mother's body. She scolded them in the following impromptu verse:

A mhná na gCathrach,
Anuas ón mBarra Ghlas,
Nach grod a tachtadh sibh!
Ní hí mo bhanaltra
A thug ón mbaile sibh
Ach tobac a's salann
I gcóir na seachtaine!

(Women of Cathracha,
Down from Barra Glas,
How quickly ye dried up!
It wasn't my dead mother
Brought ye from home
But the tobacco and salt
For the coming week!)

Since money was to be earned by these female keeners, it was but a natural step to find them, singly or in groups, in competition over the dead body, each striving to outdo the others. On such occasions, the rivals would soon desist

137

from their artificial wailings and castigate one another in bitter verse. When this happened, they would be ejected ignominously from the wake-house – a good riddance!

Just as the clergy condemned other abuses at wakes, such as drunkenness, lewd games and disorderly behaviour, so too they tried to end the hiring of keeners. The following are some of the orders issued in this connection down through recent centuries by Synods of bishops.

Synod of Tuam (1631)

Statute 3 ordered that thenceforth exaggerated crying and keening at wakes of the dead should cease[13].

Synod of Tuam (1660)

The people were advised to discontinue the practice of employing female keeners at wakes and funerals[14].

Synod of Armagh (1660)

This Synod forbade wailings and crying at funerals, as an unchristian practice[15].

Synod of Dublin (June, 1670)

This was a meeting of the archbishops and bishops of Ireland. Statute 5 ordered each priest in the country to make every effort in his power to bring to an end the wailings and screams of female keeners who accompanied the dead to the graveyard[16].

Synod of Armagh (August, 1670)

This Synod adopted the regulations laid down by the Dublin Synod two months before. It further announced that no priest would attend a wake or funeral at which female keeners cried and screamed. Any priest who neglected to endeavour to end such unseemly behaviour would be removed from his parish[17].

Synod of Meath (1686)

The bishops first condemned dancing, other amusements

and drinking at wakes, and then went on to order the parish priests in their jurisdiction to continue their efforts to put an end to the customary keening at funerals[18].

Diocese of Leighlin (1748)

Among the diocesan regulations adopted at a meeting, presided over by Most Rev. Dr. Gallagher, was the following:

'*Whereas* likewise the heathenish customs of loud cries and howlings at wakes and burials are practised amongst us, contrary to the express commandment of St. Paul in his *Epist. to the Thess.* forbidding such cries and immoderate grief for the dead, as if they were not to rise again, and to the great shame of our nation, since no such practice is found in any other Christian country; and *Whereas* in some parts of this Diocese some have the deplorable vanity in the very time of their humiliation and that God had visited them with the loss of a friend, not only to glory in the number of cries, but in order the more to feed their vanity and add fuel to their pride, do even send far and near to hire men and women to cry and compose vain fulsome rhymes in praise of their deceased friends. It is therefore *(ordained)* all Parish Priests and religious laymen of this Diocese are hereby strictly charged and commanded, in virtue of holy obedience, to use all possible means to banish from Christian burials such anti-christian practices, by imposing arbitrary punishment of prayers, fasting, alms and such like wholesome injunctions on as many men and women as will loudly cry or howl at burials. But as to such men and women as will or do make it their trade to cry or rhyme at burials, we decree and declare that for the first crime of this kind they shall not be absolved by any but by the Ordinary or his representatives, and in case of a ralapse (*sic*), the aforesaid criers or rhymers are to be excluded from Mass and the Sacraments, and in case of perseverance in this detestable practice, they are to be excommunicated and denounced[19].'

139

Sometime about the year 1800, Most Rev. Dr. Thomas Bray, Archbishop of Cashel, issued a pastoral letter which said:

'We also condemn and reprobate, in the strongest terms, all unnatural screams and shrieks, and fictitious, tuneful cries and elegies, at wakes, together with the savage custom of howling and bawling at funerals. And, in place of these pagan practices, so unmeaning, and so unbecoming Christians, we exhort all persons, who frequent wakes and funerals, rather to join, at the proper times, during the night and morning of the wake, with other pious persons, in fervent prayer, for the soul of the deceased: to comfort those that are in affliction, and in the interim also to meditate seriously on death, or otherwise to observe a becoming silence; shewing in their whole deportment a most edifying and sober gravity – which should always appear in every Christian on so awful an occasion, where the real image of death lies before his eyes. And as not only a due regard to Religion, to common decency, and for the public good, but also the ease and interest of every individual family, loudly demand that you pay all possible attention and deference to these our Pastoral instructions and regulations; we solemnly call on you, nay, we even conjure you, in the name of God, and by the authority of his holy Church, to have them most religiously observed at every wake and funeral in the several families throughout your respective parishes. Moreover, we hereby charge the consciences of all our clergy, to use their utmost zeal and vigilance, that admonitions and injunctions, so salutary and so necessary, be punctually complied with in their respective parishes. And we sincerely wish them, and all the people committed to their, and to our spiritual care, every blessing in this life and eternal happiness in the next.

N.B. The foregoing instructions and regulations, respecting wakes and funerals, are to be read once in Advent every year until they are no longer necessary; and should also be repeated as often as occasion may require, and where necessary, should also be explained in Irish[20].'

The duty of enforcing these orders fell, for the most part, on the parish priests of the various dioceses and on their curates. It was no easy task. Keening over the dead, be it real or artificial, had deep traditional roots, and country people especially were slow to abandon it. In addition to this, the paid keeners themselves were loth to discontinue a custom which was their means of livelihood. A story is told about one of these paid keening-women, who was being questioned, in a half-jocose way, about her craft; about her it was said that her wailings varied with the amount of whiskey she got. The priest had met her on the road, when she appeared to have had some drink at a wake. 'Where did the raven call today, Mary?' the priest enquired; the raven was symbolical of the banshee or Death. Mary replied in verse:

Do labhair sé thall's abhus,
Do labhair sé thiar is thoir,
Do labhair sé istigh's amuigh,
Do labhair sé i lár an toir;
Agus is duitse is fearr é sin;
Beidh airgead bán id' chrobh,
Is ór ag teacht 'na shruth;
Beidh an coirce dod' láir istigh,
Is féar breá cumhra tirim,
Is ní bhraithfir uait an puins!

(He called here and there,
He called west and east,
He called within and without,
He called in the middle of the bush;
And it was all for your benefit;
You will have silver money in your hands,
And gold coming to you in streams;
There will be oats for your horse,
And fine sweet-smelling hay,
Nor will you be short of punch!)

The priest recognised the intended insult, and said:

> *A scallaire, do chaoinfeá madra,*
> *Dá bhfaighfeá marbh é!*

(You would keen over a dog, you hag,
If you found him dead!)

Mary was still unsubdued; she replied:

> *Ní gá dhuit, 'Athair, bheith chomh searbh;*
> *Tá a haon ar an mbeo agat, is a dó ar an marbh!*

(No need for you to be so bitter, Father;
What you don't get from the living, you get from the
dead).

To this the priest rejoined:

> *Fear bruíne, bean chaointe ná garbhmhuilleoir,*
> *Ní bhfaighidh sna Flaithis aon leaba go deo.*

(Three persons who will get no bed in Heaven:
A quarrelsome man, a keening woman and a crude miller).

Mary had the word. As she noticed the priest about
to spur his horse, she said:

> *'Gaibh an bóthar caol úd soir,*
> *Nó dhéanfainnse do scrios*
> *Ó bhaitheas do chinn go troigh!'*

(Be off east along the narrow road now,
Or I'll scrape you
From the top of your head to your feet!)

Examples such as those mentioned bear witness to the
slow acceptance by both people and keeners of the orders
of the clergy, especially in the early days. Much depended
on the diligence of the priests. Neither sermons against
keening nor oral persuasion on other occasions succeeded
in breaking the custom for many centuries, especially in

remote areas. So far as I have been able to discover, female keeners ceased to be employed throughout most of Ireland towards the end of the last century; it still continued in some districts to a later date, however. My father told me that he attended a funeral in the parish of Tuosist, in South Kerry, at the turn of the century. As the coffin was being taken in a cart to the local graveyard at Kilmackillogue, three women keeners sat on top of it, howling and wailing at intervals. The parish priest, on horseback, met the funeral near Derreen, a few miles from the graveyard, and rode at its head along the road. As soon as he heard the three women howl loudly, he turned his horse about and trotted back until he reached them, where they sat on the coffin. He started to lash them with his whip, as the cart passed by, and ordered them to be silent. This they did, but on reaching the graveyard, they again took up their wailings, whereupon the priest forced them down from the coffin with his whip. They were afraid to enter the graveyard to howl at the graveside. This put an end to the hiring of keening women in that parish.

NOTES

1. See Mansi, *Collectio*, IX, 999; Bingham, *Origines Ecclesiasticae*, II, 1246.
2. Introduction, CCCXXIV.
3. Edited by Osborn Bergin, *Irisleabhar na Gaedhilge*, 6/ 1896, 18–24.
4. Ó Súilleabháin, *op. cit.*, 68–84.
5. *An Claidheamh Soluis*, 7/4/1906, 5.
6. Women keeners of the Romans (*mulieres praeficae*): Cicero, *De Legibus*, II, 23 (59); Propertius, *Elegiae*, II, 13, 27; Brand, *Pop. Antiq.*, II, 155–168; Brewer, *op. cit.*, I, CLXXXVI. Women keepers of the Greeks: Cicero, *op. cit.*; Lucian, *De luctu*, 12; Schmidt, *Die Ethnik der alten Griechen*, 114; Puckle, *op. cit.*, 112 (illustration from ancient pottery).
7. Women keeners of France: Brand, *Pop. Antiq.*, II, 167–8;

Seignolle, *op. cit.*, 88; Puckle, *op. cit.*, 68; de Nore, *op. cit.*, 93, 124. Women keeners of South-eastern Europe: Durham, *op. cit.*, 217–228 (quoting from Herodotus); Durham *loc. cit.* (Montenegro, Serbia, and Albania). Women keeners of Africa: Westermarck, *op. cit.*, II, 374–519 (*passim*). Jewish keening: Puckle, *op. cit.*, 68.

8. MacLysaght, *op. cit.*, 321–2.
9. *op. cit.*, 31.
10. *Art of Cookery*, 87.
11. There is clear evidence to show that female keeners were active in Ireland over a thousand years ago. See: An Irish Penitential (composed between 700 and 850), edited by E. F. Gwynn, *Eriú*, VII, 170–1; *The Metrical Dindshenchas*, III, 24–25, 50–51, edited by E. Gwynn (Todd Lecture Series, X); *The Rennes Dindshenchas*, edited by Whitley Stokes, *Revue Celtique*, XVI, 276–277.
12. *The Historical Works of Giraldus Cambrensis* (1186), 129; Campion, *A Historie of Ireland* (1571), 19; Derricke, *Image of Ireland* (1578), 67; Rich, *A New Description of Ireland* (1610), 12–13; do., *Irish Hubbub* (1619), 2; *Cal. of State Papers*, Ireland, James I (1611–1614), 193; Ware, *De Hibernia* (1658), 208; Piers, *Westmeath* (1682), 124; Dineley, *Observations*, (1681), 32; Eachard, *An Exact Description* (1691), 24–25; Anon., *The Comical Pilgrim's Pilgrimage to Ireland* (1723), 92; King, *Art of Cookery* (1776), 87; Campbell, *Philosophical Survey* (1778), 210–211; De Latocnaye, *A. Frenchman's Walk through Ireland* (1796–7); and the following for later times: Dutton, *Survey of Clare*, 364; Townsend, *Survey of Cork*, 90; Shaw Mason, *Parochial Survey*, I, 319, 596; *ib.*, II, 160, 367, 460, 360, 510; Dunton (third letter), MacLysaght *Irish Life in the Seventeenth Century*, 361; MacLysaght, *op. cit.*, 168, 288; Brewer, *Beauties of Ireland*, I, CLXXXV-VI; Plumtre, *Narrative*, 248, 354; Wakefield, *Ireland*, I, 597; *ib.*, II, 767, 749, 807; Elizabeth, *Sketches*, 147–151; Gamble, *A View of Society*, 329–, 332–; Rev. J. Hall, *Tour*, I, 324; *ib.*, II, 282; Beauford, *Trans. R.I. Academy*, IV; Carr, *A Stranger in Ireland*, 257–8; Blake, *Letters from the Irish Highlands*, 335, 338; Barrow, *Tour*, 346–7; Mrs. S. C. Hall, *The South and Killarney*, 87–90; Lady Wilde, *Anct. Legends*, 120; Murphy, *Slieve Gullion*, 72; Curwen, *Observations*, II, 5–6, 225–6; Gough, *Tour*, 67–8;

Binns, *Miseries and Beauties*, II, 108, 136–7; Donaldson, *Barony of Upper Fews*, 66–9; Anon., *Diary of a Tour in Ireland* (MS. 194, Nat. Library of Ireland), 27–28; Brand, *Pop. Antiq.*, II, 155–168; *Dublin Penny Journal*, I, 498, 522, 532, 548; *The Folklore Record*, IV, 100; *Béaloideas*, III, 416; *ib.*, VIII, 128; *Irish Packet*, V, 145; *Ireland's Own*, 26/3/1940, 13; *ib.*, 12/2/1955; *ib.*, XXVII, Uimh. 687, 5; *ib.*, LIX, 318; *ib.*, LXIV, 381, 631; *ib.*, LXV, 688; *An Claidheamh Soluis*, 12/6/1909, 5; Browne, *The Ethnography of Inishbofin and Inishshark*, 352–3; Browne, do. (The Mullet, Inishkea Islands and Portacloy, Co. Mayo), 623; Browne, do. (Carna and Mweenish), 522; *Seanchas Ardmhacha*, I, Uimh. 1, 124; Rodenberg, *Pilgrimage*, 186; Wood-Martin, *Elder Faiths*, I, 309–314.

13. Renehan, *Collections*, 491.
14. Renehan, *op. cit.*, 503.
15. *Spicilegium Ossoriense*, II, 200.
16. Moran, *Memoirs of Most Rev. Dr. Plunkett*, 116.
17. Renehan, *op. cit.*, 158.
18. *Archivium Hibernicum*, XX, 58.
19. Comerford, *Collections*, 81–.
20. *Stat. Synod. Cassel et Imelac* (1813), 108–.

X

CHURCH OPPOSITION
TO WAKE ABUSES

As has already been stated, there were certain aspects of
traditional wakes which drew down strong condemnation
from the Irish Church. Bishops and priests made many
attempts to curb the practices to which they objected;
strong pastoral letters were issued from time to time in
some dioceses, and bishops, on their visits to administer
Confirmation here and there, preached against the abuses.
Also when Synods of bishops of an archdiocese, or of
the whole country, met, the Statutes issued by them concerning religious matters often included one dealing with
wakes and funerals; the faithful were urged, or ordered,
to discontinue certain traditional practices; the clergy
were urged to see that the orders were carried out. This
they attempted to do, as we know from many sources,
through sermons and personal contacts down through the
centuries[1]. Here follow some examples of clerical condemnation of the manner in which wakes were conducted
in different parts of the country.

Synod of Armagh (1614)

One of the Statutes issued at this meeting deplored the
large amount of money being spent on festivities at
wakes and funerals, as well as on dark mourning clothes.
Poor people were trying to emulate the rich in these matters, thereby impoverishing succeeding generations. As
regards unseemly behaviour at wakes, the Synod declared
that the pious feelings of devout people were outraged by
the singing of lewd songs and the playing of obscene
games by silly fellows, conduct which would not be per-
missible even on occasions of merrymaking. This misbehaviour was carried on under cover of darkness; the fear

of Death was absent, although Death itself, as represented by the corpse, was before the eyes of all present. The Synod finally urged all bishops and clergy to advise their flocks on these points, and so prevent wake-houses from being places of amusement thenceforth[2].

Synod of Tuam (January, 1660)

Statute 20 of this Synod ordered all who attended Catholic wakes to abstain from excess in drink and food, from merry-making, from games and from illegal mispractices which had been introduced to lead people astray. Excesive keening by females was also condemned, and the clergy were urged to prevail upon the people to devote the money spent on wakes and funerals, or at least, the greater part of it, to Masses for the departed soul or else to alms for the poor[3].

Synod of Armagh (October 8, 1660)

Statute 15 prohibited the drinking of poteen (*aqua composita*) on occasions of matchmaking, and threatened excommunication to those who disobeyed. The same punishment, it said, would be visited on anyone who played music or danced at wakes[4].

Synod of Armagh (August 23, 1670)

Statute 2 ordered the clergy to have nothing to do with wakes or funerals, where sport and amusements were carried on by night in the wake-house – behaviour which was an insult to God and a scandal to a Catholic community. Parish priests who were negligent in endeavouring to end these abuses would be deprived of their parishes[5].

Diocese of Waterford and Lismore (1676)

Regulations for the diocese were issued after the clergy had met at Carrick-on-Suir under the chairmanship of the bishop, Most Rev. Dr. John Brenan. Statute 76 requested the clergy who might be present at wakes and funerals to ensure that Death was uppermost in the minds of those who attended; the priests were to speak quietly about this to those who were most devout and most influential in the congregation. Neither foolish talk nor exaggerated praise of the dead should be allowed. Statute 78 solemnly ordered parish priests to do all in their power to abolish all-night wakes, because of the harm done by them to souls and the dishonour shown to the God of Glory in wake-houses[6]. These and other regulations were agreed on at a meeting of the clergy of the diocese in the following year.

Synod of Meath (1686)

Statute 12 forbade dancing, amusements and the drinking of intoxicants at wakes. Statute 13 stated that, if parish priests could not end altogether night wakes and the shameful practices associated with them, it was their duty to refuse permission to attend wakes to all, except to those who were required there and the relatives of the deceased[7].

Archdiocese of Dublin (1730)

All those who had care of souls were ordered to put an end to misbehaviour at wakes, and were further to compel those who sang smutty songs or played unchristian games on these occasions to do public penance[8].

Diocese of Leighlin (1748)

The regulations for the diocese drawn up at a meeting of the bishop, Most Rev. Dr. Gallagher, and his clergy, included the following:

'Whereas also young men and women under colour of piety towards the dead, flock in crowds to wakes and watches of the dead, who, instead of being moved by the face of death painted so vividly before them on the dead corpse, or reflecting that the same night might be the last period of their unhappy lives, do abandon themselves to unchristian diversions of lewd songs, of brutal tricks

148

called fronsy fronsy or some other unlawful act of the same die and tendency. In order therefore to abolish such heathenish practices for the future, we decree and ordain –

1. That none shall be admitted to the wake of any deceased person but the family of the house wherein he is waked, or the relatives of the defunct or, at most, other grave and discreet persons.

2. We order that no clergyman whatsoever shall say Mass over the corpse of any defunct at whose wake such immodest songs, profane tricks or immoderate crowds are permitted[9]".

The regulations also condemned immoderate keening at wakes and funerals, as already mentioned in an earlier chapter.

Synod of Cashel and Emly (October 22, 1782)

Most Rev. Dr. Butler, Archbishop, presided over this meeting of bishops at Thurles, when the following Statute was among those issued:

Since the original purpose of wakes was that the soul of the deceased might be helped by the prayers of those who attended, it is evident that this purpose is being defeated when immodest games are carried on, which suppress the memory of Death in the minds of those present. We, therefore, mindful of our combined and individual authority, threaten with excommunication everybody who takes part in this evil practice henceforth. Parish priests are to forbid their congregations to cover the mouth and nostrils of the dead person until they are certain that death has actually taken place, or to bury anybody until twenty-four hours after his death[10].

Diocese of Meath (1788–1810)

Like most other bishops, Dr. Plunkett, Bishop of Meath, made a practice of preaching to the congregation in each parish of the diocese on the occasion of his annual visit. Notes left by him referring to these sermons show that he condemned abuses at wakes when he addressed the people at the following churches:

13 July, 1788 (Kilskyre); 13 October, 1789 (same); 15 August, 1790 (same); 17 August, 1792 (same); 24 June, 1797 (Ardagh and Drumconrath); 24 April, 1798 (Dromconrath); 29 July, 1798 (same); 22 July, 1805, Moynalty (in condemnation of fighting at funerals); 1809 (same venue), he spoke against travesties of the Sacraments at wakes; and 1810 (same venue) he condemned night-wakes in general[11].

Diocese of Clogher (1789)

Statute 14, issued for this diocese, urged every parish priest to endeavour to end abuses which were said to occur at wakes; also night dances, until they were completely abolished[12].

Diocese of Cashel and Emly (about 1800)

Most Rev. Dr. Thomas Bray issued a pastoral letter, which was to be read in each chapel once a year, in Advent, and as often as was necessary; it was also to be explained in Irish, if some of the congregation could not understand English:

'It being our indispensible duty to suppress by every means in our power, the very indecent practices and shameful abuses at Wakes and Funerals, which unhappily are gaining ground every day to the great prejudice and discredit of Religion, and to the disgrace and reproach of Irish Catholics; we condemn therefore, and forbid all sorts of plays and amusements at wakes, those especially against decency and modesty, and which are in mock-imitation of the sacred rites of the church, particularly in the celebration of Marriage. And by these presents we cut off, and declare cut off also by the constitutions of our dioceses, from the spiritual communion of the Church, all persons who shall assist at, promote, or otherwise be guilty of immodest plays at wakes, or of amusements wherein the ceremonies of the Church, concerning Marriage, or any other related practice are prophaned and ridiculed. And we declare that all persons who incur said spiritual censure, shall not be absolved from it, without first performing a course of exemplary penance, and by special leave from us, or from our Vicar-general, in writing.

'Moreover, we strictly charge all heads of families, not to suffer lascivious plays, or prophane amusements at wakes in their houses; otherwise they shall be considered as favouring and encouraging such abominations; and as scandalous, obstinate sinners, they are to be publicly reprimanded from the altar, and deprived also of Sacraments, until they have promised, before the congregation, never more to permit such shameful abuses in their houses[13]?

A Synod of the bishops of this diocese met ten years later, Dr. Bray presiding. Having condemned misbehaviour at 'patterns' and ordering that these festive occasions be completely banned, the Synod proceeded to remind the faithful that wakes had been instituted, in the first instance, in order that the prayers of those who attended might help the soul of the deceased. This purpose was completely lost sight of, however, where games of any kind were played at wakes, especially immodest, obscene ones which prevented those present from pondering upon Death. The clergy should, therefore, exert all their energies to root out such abuses. An end should be put to songs (*cantilenae*), to indecent talk, and especially to the very shameful game known as *Fraunces* in Ireland, in which the Sacrament of Marriage is travestied[14].

Diocese of Kildare and Leighlin (1821)

Among the Lenten regulations made by Most Rev. Dr. James Doyle, was one which forbade members of Confraternities to attend wakes[15].

Synod of the Arch-diocese of Dublin (1831)

Most Rev. Dr. Daniel Murray, Archbishop of Dublin, presided. Other bishops present were: Most Rev. Dr. James Keating (Ferns), Most Rev. Dr. James Doyle (Kildare and Leighlin) and Most Rev. Dr. William Kinsella (Ossory).

One of the Statutes called for the abolition of abuses at wakes, and of the wakes themselves in due course. The clergy were ordered to reprimand severely those who were guilty of taking part, and to advise their people to substitute prayers and spiritual readings for games of any kind. They were also to advise and order, where necessary, that burials take place either early in the morning or before noon. Young, unmarried persons were solemnly forbidden to attend wakes between sunset and sunrise, unless they were closely related to the deceased. The clergy were urged to do their utmost to see, as far as possible, that this regulation was obeyed[16].

Parish of Tydavnet, Co. Monaghan (1832)

Among the regulations in force in that parish were the following:

1. No person, male or female, who sang as a member of the parish choir, might go to a wake outside their own townland to sing or for any other purpose; those who disobeyed the order would have to leave the choir. At every wake, some good book concerning Death or Hell or Judgement or Heaven should be read.

2. No young person might attend a wake outside his own townland, except that of somebody who was a first or second cousin. Those who disobeyed this rule, or who attended an all-night dance, would be refused the Sacraments until they had made public repentance in church on a fixed Sunday[17].

Diocese of Ardagh (1834)

The bishop, Most Rev. Dr. William Higgins, announced the following regulations regarding wakes:

'We are saddened and heartbroken to learn that much

evil is resulting from rough wakes among our people, and that the behaviour of young people is being affected by them. We, therefore, request the clergy to endeavour to eradicate such abuses in their own parishes. They must point out to the parishioners that the playing of lewd games at wakes, where Death should rather be pondered on, is synonymous with turning their backs on their Faith. The clergy must take care to ensure that indecent talk and especially the sinful practice of travestying the Sacrament of Marriage are abolished on such occasions. Parish priests are to ensure that prayers are recited for the soul of the deceased and that spiritual books are read. Unmarried young men and women are solemnly forbidden to attend wakes between sunrise and sunset, with the exception of those who are related by blood or by marriage with the deceased[18].'

Synod of Armagh (October 8, 1860)
Bishops from Armagh, Meath and Kilmore met on that date at Clonelly. Among the practices condemned by them were the spilling of brandy on the ground when matchmaking, and music, singing or dancing at wakes[19].

Synod of Maynooth (1875)
At this Synod of Irish bishops, the following Statutes (357 and 358) were enacted:

'Parish priests must put an end to unchristian wakes, where the corpse is present, and where games, dances, singing and drinking are carried on – these abuses are a shame and a disgrace to the house of the dead. Parish priests must similarly ensure that only members of the family of the deceased and near relatives spend the whole night at wakes.

'During the period of the wake, prayers should be recited for the soul of the deceased and the Rosary should be said, or else spiritual books should be read, in order that those present may ponder on Death and on the shortness of life, for the benefit of their own souls.

'The Religious Societies in each parish will be able to help the soul of the dead person greatly by seeing that these things are done[20].'

Diocese of Ferns (1898)

The Statutes enacted by the bishop of this diocese in that year, so far as they dealt with wakes, were practically identical with those of the Synod of the Arch-diocese of Dublin in 1831. The bishop forbade rough games at wakes and recommended the recitation of prayers and the reading of spiritual books instead of certain games[21].

Diocese of Ardagh and Clonmacnoise (1903)

Most Rev. Dr. Hoare, bishop of the diocese, sent out an order, a copy of which was to be hung up in every chapel, forbidding unmarried men or women to attend wakes thenceforth from sunset to sunrise. Only the near relatives of the dead person were exempted. Those who disobeyed the order would be guilty of mortal sin, the bishop said, and Mass would not be celebrated in any wake-house in which the rule was broken.

Synod of Maynooth (1927)

This Synod forbade absolutely the holding of unchristian and unseemly wakes, at which the corpse was present[22].

. . . .

The afore-mentioned decrees and regulations of the bishops and clergy are but some of the many which were probably issued in Ireland in attempts to curb or end abuses at wakes and funerals. Many other episcopal Synods were also held during the past five or more centuries, whose decrees are not available to me for examination, and some, at least, of them may have referred to wakes and funerals.

Ireland was not the only country, of course, in which the Church condemned abuses at wakes and gave its flock advice concerning them. Rochholz, in his book about German folk-belief and customs (*Deutscher Glaube und*

154

Brauch), gives an account of an episcopal Synod held in Arles in France some time in the fourth or fifth century. It forbade the drinking and dancing which were associated with burials. 'These things – singing songs and carousing and such – are devilish in origin and spring neither from Christianity nor from human nature. How can love for the dead be shown by dancing on his grave?' the Synod asked. The *Indiculus Superstitionum*, a list of superstitions compiled by clerics in the year 743, indicates that the clergy at that time were actively condemning *sacrilegia ad sepulchra mortuorum* (abuses at funerals) and *sacrilegia super defunctos* (abuses over the dead); what these abuses actually were is not clear[23]. The Church, too, regarded as scandalous, the feasting, drinking and other goings-on which were in vogue throughout the greater part of Europe on certain festivals at that time, especially on the Feast of the Dead[24]. I would proffer an opinion that these continental customs, associated with the dead, may be connected with the Irish habit of leaving food outside the house at night for the dead and preparing the house for their use at night, if they came to visit. A cleric named Burchardt, of Worms, in Germany, has left us a reference dated the year 1000 or so, to 'people who sing devilish songs over the dead at wakes by night and who drink and feast there, so that one would imagine that the dead were being congratulated and rejoiced with on the occasion of their death'. He went on to say that nobody should have the audacity to sing devilish songs, or to sport or dance on such occasions[25]. Burchardt was probably referring to occurrences which were taking place round about him in Central Europe.

In north-western Europe too, the Church in Norway was displeased with wakes and with what went on at them. Reidar Th. Christiansen of Oslo has told of the efforts made by a Norwegian minister in 1741 to curb wakes and their abuses; nine years later, Bishop Pontopiddan announced that he strongly supported the clergy in this connection. Some of the Norwegian ministers did succeed in abolishing wakes in their own rural parishes, as Church statutes and enactments had succeeding in doing in towns and cities between 1640 and 1650. By the middle of the nineteenth century, wakes had altogether ceased to be held in Norway[26].

The Church in England took an equally strong stand against abuses at wakes. An episcopal Synod held in London sometime during the reign of Edward III (1312–1377) approved of a Statute or Canon (number 10), aimed at 'putting an end to the misbehaviour which took place when people assembled to wake the dead before burial. Originally people had attended wakes to pray together for the soul of the deceased. But nowadays an overgrowth of superstition and malpractice has smothered that devout custom, and wakes have degenerated into occasions for thievery and dissipation. In an endeavour to check these, we ordain that, should anybody die in a private house, no one is to be permitted to attend the wake, except the near relatives and friends of the deceased and those who promise to recite a certain number of psalms for his soul. Anybody who disobeys this regulation will be excommunicated[27]'.

The Church in Scotland enacted rules of the same nature, with the penalty of excommunication for disregarding them[28].

Here in Ireland, the burden of enforcing the episcopal decrees fell mainly, as I have said, on the shoulders of the parish priests and their curates[29]. It must have been very difficult, if not impossible, to do this effectively a few hundred years ago when priests were scarce, or in hiding, on account of the Penal laws, and when many parishes were lacking in organisation. In addition to this the ordinary people were slow to discontinue traditional customs which had been handed down to them by their forefathers. For this reason, some bishops (in the Arch-diocese of Armagh, for example) had to enact and re-enact at Synod after Synod the same Statutes condemning abuses at wakes. Hundreds of years went by before the regulations finally took effect; in the Arch-diocese of Armagh, although, as we have seen, the bishops condemned wake-abuses in 1614, in 1660, and again in 1670, wake-games in that area were still played as recently as twenty years ago! The custom was too deeply rooted to be easily eradicated.

Old people have told me that in their young days visiting priests who were engaged by the local clergy to conduct parish Missions occasionally delivered strong sermons about the type of wakes which were held in the parish. And both the local clergy and the missioners threatened to refuse absolution to those who took part in tricks and games at wakes.

Still, many people who played games themselves at wakes have told me that some of the clergy did not interfere with amusements at wakes at all. Clerical action was taken only when the games and other facets of local wakes were possible occasions for scandal; otherwise they were allowed to die out naturally with the passage of time. And this is what has happened.

NOTES

1. *Proc. R. I. Academy*, third series, III, No. 4, 622; Hartmann, *Totenkult*, 113.
2. Renehan, *op. cit.*, 144–5.
3. Renehan, *op. cit.*, 503.
4. *Spicilegium Ossoriense*, II, 199–200.
5. Renehan, *op. cit.*, 158.
6. *Spic. Ossor.*, II, 239–240.
7. *Arch. Hib.*, XX, 58.
8. Dublin, 1730.
9. Comerford, *Collections*, 81.
10. Renehan, *op. cit.*, 479.
11. Cogan, *op. cit.*, II, 205–6, 216, 223; *ib.*, III, 258, 284, 296, 340, 387.
12. *Archiv. Hib.*, XII, 66.
13. *Stat. Synod. Cassel et Imelac* (1813), 105–8.
14. *Stat. Synod. Cassel et Imelac* (1813), 72.

15. *Pastoral Instructions for the Lent of 1821*.
16. *Stat. Dioec. per Prov. Dub. observanda* (1831), 183–4.
17. *Archiv. Hib.*, XII, 69.
18. *Stat. Dioec. in Dioec. Ardacadensi observanda* (10/1834), 98–99; Hartmann, *Totenkult*, 117.
19. *Jour. Ardagh & Clonmacnoise Antiq. Soc.*, I, No. 6, 86.
20. *Acta et Decreta Syn. Plen. Episcop. Hib.*, 146.
21. *Stat. Dioec. Fernensis* (1898), 61–62.
22. *Statuta*, No. 324.
23. Grimm, *Deutsche Mythologie*, III, 405. See also, Hagberg, *op. cit.*, 241, 245–6.
24. For an account of the feasts of the dead throughout Europe, see: Christiansen, *op. cit.*, 46–87; Brand, *op. cit.*, II, 147–; Strutt, *op. cit.*, 468–.
25. Grimm, *op. cit.*, III, 405–.
26. Christiansen, *op. cit.*, 29–31.
27. Brand, *op. cit.*, II, 140–1.
28. McPherson, *op. cit.*, 125; Murray, *op. cit.*, 117.
29. Marley, *The Good Confessor*, 165; *Proc. R. I. Academy*, third series, III, No. 4, 622.

XI

THE EXTENT OF WAKE
AMUSEMENTS

Many Irish people of the present day would doubtless feel ashamed on learning that the wakes held by their not so remote forefathers were occasions for fun and frolic. But if they went on to conclude that it was only in Ireland that such merry wakes were held, they would be much mistaken. The wake, as an institution, is very ancient, and there is no lack of evidence to show that throughout a large part of Europe, feasting and drinking, dancing, singing and music were normal features of wakes as long ago as the start of the Middle Ages, about a thousand years ago. We have already read how the cleric, Burchardt of Worms, condemned devilish songs and feasting and drinking at wakes in his own day, and we have proof that the German bishops castigated the same songs, as well as the telling of funny stories and dancing at wakes. They pointed out that people should go to a wake *tremore et reverentia* (with fear of Death and respect for the dead); it was the Devil himself, they said, who had taught the pagans to sing songs on such an occasion. We have seen also that English bishops were forced to take action against wake-abuses in their own dioceses six hundred years ago.

It is very difficult, if not almost impossible, to find accounts of the way of life of the common people in olden times. While we are well-documented for so-called official history (wars, Acts of Parliament and such), historians and chroniclers have not thought it worthwhile to record social conditions at all. This means that much time and patience is entailed by a search in scattered sources for this type of information, often with disappointingly meagre results. Of wakes in Europe six centuries ago, we

159

would have hardly any accounts, were it not that a series of plagues spread through the continent at that time, such as the Plague of 1349 or so. In recording the many deaths and general misery caused by these plagues, some contemporary writers of the period have occasionally referred to the wakes held over the dead and the amusements associated with them. Paetorius[1] has described the wakes of the period around 1662; and contemporary reports from Germany and the Transylvanian part of Hungary also help to fill in the picture[2]. The Statutes of episcopal Synods which met in Europe in past centuries and condemned wake-festivities, among other abuses, help to balance what we know from oral sources.

Courtship and love-making were normal features of old-time wakes in Germany and Scandinavia[3]. Storytelling, especially the narration of humorous tales, was common also[4]. We have many accounts of lewd games played at continental wakes, and of dances performed around the coffin, especially if the dead person were young. In Westphalia, on such occasions, the young people at the wake would select a young fellow or girl to lie down on the floor, representing, as it were, the deceased. In the case of a boy, the girls would bend over him, one by one, kiss him and start to sing and dance around him. This type of ring-dance was common at wakes in German Silesia and in Hungary[5].

Games were played at wakes throughout the greater part of Europe: from Ireland in the west, through Hungary and Roumania, to the Ukraine in Russia, and from Scandinavia in the north to Italy in the south[6]. Nor was the custom confined to Europe alone: wakes in Mexico, in the territories of the Red Indians of the United States, and in the islands of the Pacific Ocean were all occasions for merrymaking and amusement[7].

In Europe, the Christian Church endeavoured to get the people to sing psalms and prayers at wakes[8], instead of the usual love-songs. Other features of wakes, such as the playing of cards and other games, as well as drinking, lasted for many centuries in other countries, as they did in Ireland.

We have already seen that Irish wakes, before our own days, were traditionally merry occasions; people feasted and drank, played many types of games, told stories, sang and danced. So far as I have been able to determine, southwest Cork and southwest Kerry differed in this respect from the rest of the country, since in that rather restricted area, storytelling was the only known type of entertainment at wakes; the only exceptions to this, which I have been able to find, were the playing of a game at a wake in the Iveragh peninsula and near Killarney, both in Kerry. Elsewhere in Ireland, games were played generally at wakes of elderly people, and merrymaking went on, even in Dublin City, where, as we have seen, some games were played at wakes as recently as forty years ago[9]. So too, wake-games were played in the town of Wexford; and Coulter has described how wakes in Belfast were occasions for drinking and merrymaking[10].

Protestant wakes seem to have been outside the scope of wake-games, so far as I know. Psalms were sung, however[11].

Even when the Irish emigrated to other countries, they took with them many of their customs, moulded by their traditional way of thinking. Thus, so far as we know, Irish wakes abroad resembled a good deal those held in the homeland. Coulter has given a description of the wake of an Irishman in Wolverhampton, where songs were sung and drinks provided[12]. So too, we have an account of the money spent by Irish and Scottish emigrants on provisions for the wake of a man who was drowned in New Hampshire, in the United States, in the year 1678[13]. There is a dearth of information about the wakes of Irishmen who died among their own kith and kin abroad, but, in some aspects, at least, many of the old home customs must have been observed.

When one examines the kinds of amusements current at old-time wakes, one finds that they belonged to the general pattern of pastimes in vogue among the people[14]. Feasting, drinking, and the use of snuff were usual, wherever the occasion suited. So too, storytelling, riddling, verse-making and the many games already described were popular on many other occasions, apart from wakes, where people met. What may now strike us as odd, if not as disgraceful, is that some of these pastimes should be indulged in beside the corpse in a wake-house. For our forefathers generally, however, a wake had altogether a different meaning from what it has for us today. Tradition was strong enough to stifle any feeling of guilt or shame they might otherwise have felt because of the unseemly conduct at wakes. They went to wakes to enjoy themselves; and old people have told me that in the old days the wake of an old person was a far merrier and more enjoyable occasion than even a wedding.

It is regrettable that no compilation has yet been made of the traditional games and other forms of amusement which were popular among the Irish people down through the centuries. A book, or a series of volumes on this interesting subject, is badly needed in this country. The lack of such a work makes it very difficult to examine objectively the games and other amusements used at wakes. Where did they originate? When and how did they spread through Ireland? These are questions not easy to answer. I have gone through helpful compilations from other countries, such as those made by Strutt, Halliday, Sutton-Smith and Brand, as well as the collection of games made by Alice Gomme. I have also examined the list of Swedish games and amusements, *Idrottslekar*, to try to find analogies to any or all of our Irish wake-games. Although the foreign compilers just mentioned were not concerned at all with wake-games — merely with games — still I found that eighty games mentioned by Alice Gomme (as parlour-games) were played at Irish wakes; so too were twentyone listed by Sutton-Smith from New Zealand, and twentythree from Sweden. In smaller lists of games from other countries, I found just a few which were popular at Irish wakes.

I think that it may fairly be said that the majority of, if not all, games played at wakes in this country belonged to the stock of general popular amusements. It is unlikely that any of them were specially invented for wakes alone. While varying locally somewhat in details, the games-repertoire of most countries forms part of a widespread pattern. To revert to wake-games, it is known that such trials of strengh as Pulling the Stick and Lifting by the Hough, which I have described earlier, were also normal tests among the young men of Sweden in olden times. A number of the games which Louise Hagberg has said were played at Swedish wakes were popular on similar occasions here in Ireland. In his description of wake-games in the Ukraine of Russia[15], Samuel Koenig mentions one which was very common at Irish wakes, and bears out the reason for the games given by old people here – to help to keep those attending the wake from falling asleep.

It is probable that some, at least, of our popular amusements at wakes and generally, are native to this country. Others were introduced at various times from England and Scotland, two countries with which Ireland has had long associations in different fields. Travelling labourers (*spailpíní*), who emigrated in their thousands seasonally to Great Britain, as well as soldiers and sailors serving abroad, and the countless other travellers and returning emigrants must all have helped to bring many facets of foreign culture, including games, into Ireland. Once they took root here, they were spread in due course over the whole country by *spailpíní*, 'poor scholars', servant boys and girls, poor travelling folk, and the normal social contacts of people.

Although Ireland can boast of having the oldest written literature in Western Europe, and although our *corpus* of old manuscripts, despite our troubled history and the losses it entailed, is impressive, still one searches almost in vain for any straight-forward descriptions of the way

163

in which the ordinary people lived – or died. Nothing is known for certain about how the dead were waked, say, a thousand years ago. We can only suppose that, owing to the tenacity of traditional customs, the wakes at that time differed only in detail from those which have lasted down to almost our own day. It is only since the sixteenth century, however, that printed sources give us any information about wakes and funerals, which often drew down condemnation from bishops during that century and the succeeding ones, as we have seen.

The rhythm of social behaviour is subject to constant change, and wakes, like other aspects of life, have been influenced by the passage of time. The lively, merry, boisterous wakes of former years have almost totally disappeared; only their memory remains. New ideas, new ways of thinking and, above all, the influence of the Church have all been involved in their ending. The more or less continual barrage of episcopal condemnation of abuses slowly, but surely, achieved its purpose. The *Irish Catholic Directory*[16] for the years 1845 to 1847, in a statement on the position of religion in the Diocese of Clonfert, described how the bishop had shortly before established a Purgatorial Society, which had succeeded in putting an end to wake-abuses in the diocese; the clergy often called upon lay assistance in that way to solve particular local problems. Similarly, the *Parliamentary Gazeteer of Ireland*[17] announced in 1846 that shameful wakes were abolished in rural areas. This was only partly true, as other evidence proves. In the middle of the last century, wakes were waning in Scandinavia also.

As I have already stated wakes in my native parish of Tuosist, in South Kerry, had always been, so far as I know, decorous and solemn occasions, with storytelling as the only form of entertainment. Still, I well remember that, on the day when I was confirmed along with other children over fifty years ago, the bishop of Kerry devoted his allocution to the congregation to advising them, when somebody died, to bring the corpse to the local church the evening before the interment. Many bishops throughout Ireland had been urging this during previous decades, and when people conformed, the wake thenceforth lasted for one night only. It would then be a rather small wake, with very little, if any, feasting or drinking, and those who attended would be much fewer than would be the case on the following night. When one-night wakes became general, the games and other festivities ceased, as they demanded that the corpse be present; now it was in the local church awaiting burial next day.

Wakes, as social institutions, have long since ceased throughout the greater part of Europe. They now survive in an attenuated form only here in Ireland[18], and, possibly, a few other scattered areas of Western Europe.

NOTES

1. *Philosophia colus* (1662), 219.
2. *Hwbch. des d. Abergl.*, V, 1106.
3. Hagberg, *op. cit.*, 239–246; *Hwbch. des d. Abergl.*, V, 1110.
4. *Hwbch. des d. Abergl.*, V, 1110.
5. Hagberg, *op. cit.*, 239–246, 445–8; *Hwbch. des d. Abergl.*, V, 1110–1111.
6. Hagberg, *op. cit.*, 239–246; *Hwbch. des d. Abergl.*, *loc. cit.*
7. Hagberg, *loc. cit.*; *Hwbch. des d. Abergl.*, *loc. cit.*; *Jour. Kilk. Arch. Soc.*, II, 333–4.
8. Christiansen, *op. cit.*, 62.
9. *The Bell*, III, 313; *Salmagundi*, 22/2/1834.
10. *Curious Notions*, 58.
11. Lynd, *Home Life*, 110.
12. *op. cit.*, 59.
13. Earle, *Customs and Fashions*, 364–.
14. Gomme, *Trad. Games*; Sutton-Smith, *op. cit.*; Brand, *op. cit.*; *Idrottslekar*.
15. *Folk-Lore* (1946), 86.
16. 1845, 273; 1846, 325; 1847, 344.
17. I (1846), 49.
18. Christiansen, *op. cit.*, 31.

XII

THE ORIGIN AND PURPOSE OF WAKES AND THEIR AMUSEMENTS

The time is now appropriate to ask some questions – and to look for possible answers. What was the original purpose of wakes? Why the feasting and drinking? Why the games and lively entertainments? Why the immoderate keening? Why the long procession of customs and superstitions associated with wakes and funerals, and with death generally?

Let us take the first question: What was the original purpose of wakes? Seen from our present-day standpoint, they must have been intended to offer relatives, friends and neighbours an opportunity of visiting the wake-house to offer their sympathy and help to the bereaved family and to pray for the deceased. Why the feasting and drinking? These too would seem to be reasonable: people who attended a wake might need some food and drink, if they stayed for a long time, or if they had travelled a long distance. But why the games and lively entertainments? To us today, such conduct in the presence of the corpse and of the relatives would be regarded as thoughtless and shameful; many of the present generation would find it hard to believe that what I have described in this book ever took place in any country, least of all in Ireland, and finding that it did, would thank God that it no longer existed. Other customs and superstitions which are called into play at a time of death, even at the present time, would be quietly accepted as traditional, strange though many of them seem nowadays.

I have asked several people who took part in various wake-amusements in former times why they did so. Four main reasons were given:

(*a*) It was a traditional custom, handed down by their forefathers, and no harm was caused by carrying it on.

(*b*) It was a widespread custom in many districts, and no wake-house wished to be different from the general pattern.

(*c*) The games and other amusements were carried on in order to pass away the long night until morning[1].

(*d*) The games helped to keep people awake, especially after midnight[2].

All of these reasons given by people who are still alive sound sensible and rather hard to object to. The hold of tradition over people, especially in rural areas, was strong; nobody wishes to be regarded as 'odd man out' in a small community; and amusements of some kind help to pass the time and prevent people from dozing to sleep in company.

A city man, with whom I have discussed the matter, offered his opinion that the liveliness and merrymaking at wakes were a kind of defiant gesture by those who took part, to show that, unlike the corpse, which lay dead in their presence, they were still 'alive and kicking', and set out to prove it. That suggestion too has a certain amount of logic in it. Still, I doubt whether it solves the problem of the gaiety and entertainment at old-time wakes.

Many scholars and writers have written books in different languages about the probable origin of the wake as an institution. Some have advanced the theory that the wake was intended as a protection for the dead person against evil spirits. It must be admitted that there is no lack of stories about corpses which vanished on different occasions, and the blame for such happenings has been variously laid at the doors of doctors (who, in the earlier years of medicine, experimented on newly-dead corpses), the Devil himself, ghosts or evil spirits of some kind. Stories of this kind hardly help to solve the problem of the origin of the wake, however. Other researchers have suggested that the wake was intended to ensure that the person concerned was really dead before being buried. The seeming onset of death might be caused by a prolonged faint, for example, or by some unusual illness, and, if allowed sufficient time, the patient might recover consciousness; hence, the wake, they said. It was a reasonable solution, in its own way, but it hardly tells the whole story.

The problem of the origin of wakes still remained unsolved, so far as I was concerned. Then about fifteen years ago, I received from my friend in Oslo, Professor Reidar Th. Christiansen, a signed copy of a book by him which had just been published. Its title was *The Dead and the Living*. As I read it, I immediately realised that I had found at last the best explanation of all to account, not only for the wake itself in its origin, but also for the fun and games associated with it. In his book, Professor Christiansen did not even refer to Irish wakes or to their accompanying amusements. His subject was, rather, that part of the field of folk belief and custom which dealt with relations between the dead and the living. He was mainly concerned with the traditional position in north-western Europe, with illustrations from areas further afield to support his thesis. His basic theory, as stated in this interesting volume, seemed so rational and soundly-based, to my mind, that I wish to summarise it here, as it solves, for myself, at least, the problems connected with our old Irish wakes and what took place at them.

The professor first comments on the general nature of folklore, more especially of folk belief and custom. These two run like a pair of threads through the web of traditional lore which has been handed down to all people through the ages. Many scholars, he says, have devoted much time and energy to the study of folklore in attempts to get information about the growth, development and history of the human race, without always realising that some aspects of this lore are much younger than others. Folklore, he continues, is an amalgam of various ideas and practices of many different origins, each arising in its own way and time. Some are derived from pagan times, while others are blended with Christianity and influenced by it. The professor regards folklore as a kind of stream, at the bottom of which runs a strong current which directs our minds and thoughts in a certain direction and, at the same time, prevents us from too easily accepting any and every new idea which crops up. It is this hidden current which gives uniform colour to folk customs the world over, differing though they do in detail. These folk practices do not belong to any single age; rather have they been derived from every age since man was first created down to our own day. They help to safeguard human life and prosperity, and it is only natural that they come more into play at times of human crisis than on other occasions. It will not surprise us, therefore, to learn that Death, the supreme, crucial crisis in human affairs, was surrounded by a formidable array of folk custom and belief.

People of modern generations are inclined to look a-skance at old customs and beliefs (so-called superstitions) and to regard them as foolish and nonsensical. Be that as it may, it is a wrong approach. These old beliefs and practices are worthy of sympathetic and careful study. They were items in the traditional code of behaviour of our ancestors – may of them as old as, if not older than, the earliest stone monument in Ireland – and were earnest attempts, under primitive conditions, to safeguard human life and interests against attacks from unseen, therefore, possibly evil, outside forces. Like the traffic code of our day, these so-called superstitions were realistic rules of conduct and behaviour in their own day. Now outmoded, their main value is to give us an insight into the mind and ways of thinking of our forefathers in times gone by.

As Christians, it is difficult for us to imagine how people in pagan times regarded Death and what might follow it. They knew by experience that Death ended the normal way of life which the deceased had known. Still, they believed that, in some way or another, 'life' of some kind continued beyond the grave. Christianity taught them gradually about the existence of the human soul which was not ended by Death; nevertheless they felt that the dead were still involved in some way in human affairs, still continuing in some kind of human form which was rather like that held during life.

The main feeling of the living towards the dead in early times all over the world was one of fear. C. E. Vulliamy has expressed it thus[3]: 'And just as a common experience has inculcated the belief in the immortal, so a common sentiment has united men in their attitude towards the dead: the sentiment of fear. It is fear that seals the sepulchre, fear that binds or maims the body, fear that fills the grave with treasured property or with the victims of cruel sacrifice. It is through fear that man takes up the attitude of worship and seeks to propitiate the watchful and terrible dead. By vision born of fear men know the horrors of darkness, and by that vision they bear testimony to ghostly visions and ghostly actions. Through exceeding fear the dead are raised, first to the plane of the living and then above it; and so it is along a pathway of fear that man approaches his hard-faced gods... It is not easy for us to believe that the mental evolution of man leads him through a stage where the dead are the absolute lords and masters of the living.'

That fear of the dead was one of the main strands running through primitive religions of all kinds is amply illustrated by the series of lectures of Sir James Fraser, *The Fear of the Dead in Primitive Religion*. It is still operative among peoples who have not been fully integrated into the Christian Faith. Even professed christians of our own day are influenced by fear of the unknown. Who among us is not afraid of meeting a ghost or seeing something uncanny late at night?

For primitive peoples, there was no real boundary between this life and the next, if such existed – and they believed that it did. It took the teachings of Christianity hundreds of years to penetrate and change the older attitudes. Even today, traces of the old way of thinking are easily discernible even in Ireland.

Why should the living have feared the dead in earlier times? Their first attitude towards one who had died was one of pity, as friends and property had to be left behind for some reason which was not quite clear to them. This feeling of pity was mixed with a still stronger feeling of fear that the dead person might return to take revenge on those who had succeeded to his property. Thus the survivors did everything in their power to placate the dead. This could best be done while the dead body was still with them. Hence the wake. It was originally intended to give the living a chance of showing goodwill towards the dead and of sympathising with him in his decease. By doing this, they hoped to gain his own goodwill and thus negative any evil dispositions he might have towards them. By showing, as it were, that the dead person was still one of themselves, and by rallying around him to bid a last farewell, they hoped to placate his anger towards them. That is why all who attended the wake gave him a good send-off by a party in his honour.

As well as the fear held by the living of possible revenge by the dead, there was an additional fear that the dead were always anxious to take living persons off into the otherworld[4] From this arose the widespread fear of ghosts and other beings from outside this world of ours. Thousands of stories have been collected about people who, in their youth and full vigour, were frightened at night by some ghostly spectre, barely succeeded in returning home, took to their beds and died within a short time. That the so-called vision was the result of hallucination or some normal cause, and that death occurred as the natural consequence of some bodily ailment, was never admitted, if thought of at all. No, the person who died rather suddenly in these circumstances had been taken off into the otherworld by the inimical dead.

Thus the wake originally concentrated on showing sym-

171

pathy for the dead, not for his relatives. It was an attempt to heal the wound of Death, and to do final justice to the deceased while he was still physically present. After the burial, the opportunity to do so would be absent. That is why both relatives and friends strove to show that Death was but a trivial occurrence, which could be alleviated by all the features of the wake: the feasting and drinking, the attendance at the wake-house, the fun and amusements, and even the keening. The great occasion was in honour of the deceased alone, and he was the one and only guest. We can more easily understand, if we remember this view-point, why cards were put into the hands of the corpse, or a pipe into his mouth[5], or why, on some occasions, the dead was taken out on the floor to join in the dance. He had to be assured of his popularity and of his continuing presence as one of the company. Any untoward behaviour or disrespect towards the corpse, which might occur at some wakes, can be explained by the passage of time which had blurred and submerged the original purpose of the wake as an institution.

Adherence to the traditional pattern of wakes helped to ease the burden of sorrow of the relatives too. They felt better for carrying on the practice of their ancestors; and when all was over, they felt proud at having acted as their deceased forefathers would have wished[6].

The old ways have now yielded place to the new, and not only the probable origin of the wake but even memory of its attendant practices are things of the past. This is not to be deplored, as Christianity has taught us to look upon Death as but a gateway to a better life. Prayers and seemly behaviour now take the place of the robust games of former days, and feasting and drinking are confined to a minimum. Drunkenness at wakes is unknown in these times, and young people no longer use the occasion for showing off their prowess or cleverness.

As previously stated, the wake was the last occasion on which the dead and the living could share each other's company. The latter regarded it as an important function, and they were sure that the dead looked upon it in the same way. This is evident from accounts which have come down to us about certain aspects of wakes here and there in Europe[7]. Before the corpse was taken out of the house for the last time, all present sat down together to share a meal in his presence. In Norway, as the corpse lay in the uncovered coffin in the kitchen, while the meal was being eaten, old women would address the deceased, saying: 'Now you will take this last meal in our company[8].' In Norway also, when the coffin had been taken outside the house and placed on the cart or sledge for removal to the graveyard, a pause took place. A large bowl of beer was placed on the lid of the coffin, and its contents were shared out among those present, as if it were a gift from the corpse. Then, when it had been drunk, some fluent speaker in the company stood forward and thanked those present, in the name of the dead person, for the good wake they had given him; the speaker might be a relative or friend or somebody else who was capable of acting the part[9]. The same ceremony took place also in other countries: in Bohemia, in Prussia, In Denmark and in Sweden. It was also carried out in England in the seventeenth century[10]. Although this feature of the wake is not known to have been practised in Ireland, there is no lack of stories about those dead who returned to complain about the neglect in carrying out some traditional custom at the time of their decease. Both pagandom and Christianity were agreed on one thing: the dead were still the concern of the living whether in the otherworld of pagan belief or in Purgatory.

Finally, I think that is is possible to make a connection and comparison between wake-games and associated amusements, on the one hand, and what went on at the great fairs (at Teltown, for example) which were held at certain places in ancient Ireland, on the other. Professor D. A. Binchy, in his article about The Fair of Tailtiu and the Feast of Tara, says: 'From several statements in the Laws (e.g. Críth Gablach 500 f., etc.) it is clear that the king of every tribe was bound to convene an *óenach* at regular intervals. The site of the fair was normally an ancient burial ground: indeed the tradition reflected in many poems and sagas that the *óenach* originated in the funeral games held for kings and heroes may have a kernel of truth[11].' It would not be rash, to my mind, to see a basic connection between these funeral games in both Ireland and Greece, on the one hand, and the amusements carried on in humble wake-houses in Ireland and elsewhere, on the other. The game at a wake, as well as the keening, are descended from the same ultimate source as the *cluiche caointeach*[12] (game of lamentation?) which took place when a great warrior died in ancient Ireland.

NOTES

1. Shaw Mason, *op. cit.*, II, 365.
2. Wakefield, *Ireland*, II, 807; *Folk-Lore*, (1946), 86–87.
3. *Immortal Man*, 73; Westermarck, *Origin and Development*, II, 531–; Lips, *op. cit.*, 364–5.
4. Christiansen, *op. cit.*, 15–.
5. For a pipe in the mouth of the corpse, see Hartmann, *Totenkult*, 112.
6. Christiansen, *op. cit.*, 26.
7. Hagberg, *op. cit.*, 307–310.
8. Christiansen, *op. cit.*, 34; Westermarck, *Ritual and Belief*, II, 475; *Anthol. Hib.*, 12/1794, 435–6.
9. Christiansen, *op. cit.*, 34–.
10. Burne, *op. cit.*, 307.
11. *Eriú*, XVIII, 124.
12. Wood-Martin, *Elder Faiths*, I, 302–; O'Curry, *op. cit.*, I, cccxxiii–iv; Lord Walter Fitzgerald, *Jour. Kildare Arch. Soc.*, III, 2–3.

SOURCES
(a) Books

—: *Drinking to the Dead* (Halliday Pamphlet 31, R. I. Academy).

—: *The Comical Pilgrim's Pilgrimage into Ireland*. London 1723.

—: *An Amusing Summer-Companion to Glanmire near Cork*. Cork, 1814.

—: *The Irishman at Home*. Dublin, 1849.

—: *Diary of a Tour in Ireland* (MS. 194, Nat. Library of Ireland).

'An Connachtach Bán': *Na Spiadóirí agus Sgéalta eile*. Dublin, 1934.

An Irishman: *Scenes and Incidents in Irish Life*. Montreal, 1884.

Banim, Michael: *Father Connell*. London, 1849.

Barrow, John: *A Tour Round Ireland*. London, 1836.

Bell, Dr. Robert: *A Description of the Condition and Manners of the Peasantry of Ireland* (1780–1790). London, 1804.

Bingham, J.: *Origines Ecclesiasticae*. London, 1821–1829.

Binns, J.: *The Miseries and Beauties of Ireland*, I–II. London, 1837.

Blake: *Letters from the Irish Highlands*. London, 1825.

Bottrell, William: *Traditions and Hearthside Stories of West Cornwall*. Penzance, 1870.

Bourgchier, Sir Henry: *Advertisements for Ireland*, 1623 (ed. by George O'Brien). Dublin, 1923.

Brand, J.: *Observations on Popular Antiquities*, 1–II. London, 1841.

Brewer, J.: *The Beauties of Ireland*, I–II. London, 1825.

Burne, Charlotte Sophia: *Shropshire Folklore*. London, 1883.

Cambrensis, Giraldus: *Historical Works* (ed. by Th. Wright). London, 1892.

Campbell, T.: *A Philosophical Survey of the South of Ireland*. Dublin, 1778.

Campion, Edward: *A Historie of Ireland* (1571). Dublin, 1633, 1809.

Carbery, Mary: *The Farm by Lough Gur*. London, 1937.

Carleton, William: *Traits and Stories of the Irish Peasantry*. London, 1854.

Carment, Samuel: *Glimpses of the Olden Time*. Edinburgh, 1893.

Carr, J.: *A Stranger in Ireland*. London, 1806.

Christiansen, Reidar Th.: *The Dead and the Living*. Oslo, 1946 (*Studia Norvegica*, 2).

Cogan, Rev. A.: *The Diocese of Meath*, I–III. Dublin, 1862–'70.

Comerford, Rev. M.: *Collections Relating to the Diocese of Kildare and Leighlin*. Dublin, 1883.

Cooper Foster, Jeanne: *Ulster Folklore*. Belfast, 1951.

Coulter, John: *Curious Notions*. Belfast, 1890.

Courtney, M. A.: *Cornish Feasts and Folklore*. Penzance, 1890.

Croker, Thomas Crofton: *Researches in the South of Ireland*. London, 1824.

„   „   „   : *The Keen in the South of Ireland*. London, 1844.

„   „   „   : *Legends of the Lakes*. London, 1829.

Curwen, J. C.: *Observations on the State of Ireland*. London, 1818.

De Latocnaye: *A Frenchman's Walk Through Ireland*. Dublin, c. 1917.

de Nore, Alfred: *Coutumes, Mythes et Traditions des Provinces de France*. Paris, 1846.

Derricke, John: *Image of Irlande* (1578). Edinburgh, 1883.

Dineley, Thomas: *Observations in a Tour through the Kingdom of Ireland* (1681). Dublin, 1858.

Donaldson, John: *A Historical and Statistical Account of the Barony of Upper Fews in the County of Armagh*. Dundalk, 1923.

Douglas, Norman: *London Street Games*. London, 1916.

Dunton, John: Letters (MacLysaght, *Irish Life in the Seventeenth Century*, appendix).

Durham, M. E.: *Some Tribal Origins, Laws and Customs of the Balkans*. London, 1928.

Dutton, Hely: *Statistical Survey of the County of Clare*. Dublin, 1808.

Eachard, Laurence: *An Exact Description of Ireland*. London, 1691.

Earle, Alice Morse: *Customs and Fashions in Old New England.* London, 1893.

Edgeworth, Maria: *Castle Rackrent.* London, 1810.

Elizabeth, Charlotte: *Sketches of Irish History.* Dublin, 1844.

Evans, E. Estyn: *Irish Folk Ways.* London, 1957.

Farewell, James: *The Irish Hudibras.* London, 1689.

Frazer, Sir James: *The Fear of the Dead in Primitive Religion.* London, 1934.

G. J.: *Original Legends and Stories of Ireland.* Dublin, 183–.

Gamble, J.: *A View of Society and Manners in the North of Ireland.* London, 1813.

Gluckman, Max: *Rituals of Rebellion in South-east Africa.* The Frazer Lecture, 1952 (1954).

Goldsmith, Oliver: *The Vicar of Wakefield.* London, 1904.

Gomme, Alice Bertha: *The Traditional Games of England, Scotland and Ireland,* 1–II. London, 1894.

Gomme, G. L.: *English Traditions and Foreign Customs.* London, 1885.

Gough, John: *A Tour in Ireland.* Dublin, 1817 (?)

Grant, I. F.: *Everyday Life on an Old Highland Farm* (1769–1782). London, 1924.

Grimm: *Deutsche Mythologie,* I–III. Berlin, 1875–1878.

Guthrie, E. J.: *Old Scottish Customs.* London, 1885.

Hagberg, Louise: *När Döden Gäster.* Stockholm, 1937.

Hall, Rev. J.: *Tour Through Ireland,* I–II. London, 1813.

Hall, Mr. and Mrs. S. C.: *Ireland,* I–III. London, 1841.

„   „   „   : *The South and Killarney.* London, 1853.

Hartmann, Hans: *Der Totenkult in Irland.* Heidelberg, 1952.

„   „   : *Über Krankheit, Tod und Jenseitsvorstellungen in Irland.* Halle (Saale), 1942.

Henderson, W.: *Notes on the Folklore of the Northern Counties of England and the Borders.* London, 1866.

Houston, Mrs.: *Twenty Years in the Wild West.* London, 1879.

John, Alois: *Sitte, Brauch und Volksglaube im deutschen Weltböhmen.* Prag, 1905.

Kennedy, Patrick: *The Banks of the Boro.* London, 1867.

„   „   : *Evenings in the Duffrey.* Dublin, 1869.

King, W.: *Art of Cookery,* I–III. London, 1776.

Le Fanu, W. R.: *Seventy Years of Irish Life.* London, 1893.

Lips, Julius E.: *The Origin of Things.* London, 1949.

Little, George: *Malachi Horan Remembers.* Dublin, 1943.

Lover, Samuel: *Ireland Illustrated*. Dublin, 1844.

Lynd, Robert: *Home Life in Ireland*. London, 1909.

MacDonagh, Michael: *Irish Life and Character*. London, 1899.

MacDonald, Alexander: *Story and Song from Loch Ness-side*. Inverness, 1914.

MacDonald, Colin: *Echoes of the Glen*. Edinburgh, 1936.

Mac Giollarnáth, Seán: *Annála Beaga as Iorras Aithneach*. Dublin, 1941.

Mackay, William: *Urquhart and Glenmoristan*. Inverness, 1914.

Mackintosh, Sir Eneas: *Notes on Strathdearn*.

MacLysaght, Edward: *Irish Life in the Seventeenth Century*. Dublin, 1939.

MacManus, Seamus: *The Rocky Road to Dublin*. New York, 1938.

McPherson, J. M.: *Primitive Beliefs in the North-east of Scotland*. London, 1929.

Mansi, G. D.: *Sacrorum Conciliorum nova et amplissima Collectio*, XXV. Paris, 1724–1733.

Marley, Rev. Martin: *The Good Confessor*. Doway, 1743.

Marshall, J.: *Popular Rhymes and Sayings of Ireland*.

Migne: *Patrologia latina*.

Moran, Rev. P. F.: *Memoirs of Most Rev. Dr. Plunkett*. Dublin, 1861.

Murphy, M. J.: *At Slieve Gullion's Foot*. Dundalk, 1940.

Murray, Eunice G.: *Scottish Women in Bygone Days*. Glasgow, 1930.

O'Connell, Philip: *The Diocese of Kilmore*. Dublin, 1937.

O'Curry, Eugene: *Manners and Customs of the Ancient Irish*. London, 1873.

Ó Fotharta, Domhnall: *Siamsa an Gheimhridh*. Dublin, 1892.

Olofsson, Klas: *Folkliv och Folkminne*. Göteborg, 1931.

Ó Muirgheasa, Énrí: *Greann na Gaedhilge*. Dublin, 1902.

Opie, Peter: *The Lore and Language of Schoolchildren*. Oxford, 1959.

Ó Ruadháin, Seán: *Pádhraic Mháire Bhán*. Dublin, 1936.

Ó Súilleabhán, Seán: *Diarmuid na Bolgaighe*. Dublin, 1937.

O'Sullivan, Donal: *Songs of the Irish*. Dublin, 1960.

Owen, Trefor M.: *Welsh Folk Customs*. Cardiff, 1959.

Pennant, T.: *Tour in Scotland*. London, 1776.

Piers, Sir Henry: *A Chorographical Description of the County of Westmeath*. Dublin, 1770.

Plummer, Charles: *Vitae Sanctorum Hiberniae*. Oxford, 1910.

Plumtre, Anne: *Narrative of a Residence in Ireland*. London 1817.

Power, Rev. Patrick: *A Bishop of the Penal Times*, Cork, 1932.

Puckle, Bertram: *Funeral Customs*. London, 1926.

Ramsay, Dean: *Reminiscences of Scottish Life and Character*. London, no date.

Renehan, Rev. Laurence: *Collections on Irish Church History*. Dublin, 1861.

Rich, Barnaby: *A New Description of Ireland*. London, 1610.
　　　"　　　　" : *Irish Hubbub*. London, 1619.

Rodenberg, Julius: *A Pilgrimage Through Ireland*. London, 1860.

Rosén, H.: *Om Dödsrike och Dödsbruk i fornordisk Religion*. Lund, 1918.

Schmidt,–.: *Die Ethik der alten Griechen*. Berlin, 1882.

Seignolle, C. and J.: *Le Folklore du Hurepoix*. Paris, 1937.

Shaw Mason, W.: *Parochial Survey of Ireland*, I–II. Dublin, 1814.

Simpson, Eve Blantyre: *Folklore in Lowland Scotland*. London, 1908.

Skith, Mrs.: *Memoirs of a Highland Lady*.

Stewart, Alexander: *A Highland Parish, or the History of Fortingall*. Glasgow, 1928.

Strutt, Joseph: *Sports and Pastimes*. London, 1838.

Sutton-Smith, Brian: *The Games of New Zealand Children*. Folklore Studies, 12: University of California, 1959.

Townsend, Rev. Horatio: *Statistical Survey of the County Cork*. Dublin, 1810.

Vulliamy, C. E.: *Immortal Man*. London, 1926.

Wakefield, Edward: *An Account of Ireland*, I–II. London, 1812.

Waldron, G: *Description of the Isle of Man*. Douglas, 1865.

Walker, J.: *Historical Memoirs of the Irish Bards*. Dublin, 1786.

Walter, L. E.: *The Fascination of Ireland*. London, 1913.

Ware, Sir James: *De Hibernia et Antiquitatibus ejus Disquisitiones*. London, 1658.

Westermarck, Edward: *The Origin and Development of the Moral Ideas*. London, 1906.
　　　"　　　　　　　" : *Ritual and Belief in Morocco*. London, 1926.

Wilde, Lady: *Ancient Legends of Ireland*. London, 1888.

  „   „   : *Ancient Cures, Charms and Usages of Ireland*. London, 1890.

Wilde, Sir William: *Irish Popular Superstitions*. Dublin, 1853.

Wood-Martin, W.: *History of Sligo*. Dublin, 1892.

  „   „   : *Traces of the Elder Faiths of Ireland*, I–II. London, 1902.

(b) Journals and other Sources

Acta et Decreta Synodi Plenariae Episcoporum Hiberniae (1875). Dublin, 1877.

Africa. Kiltegan.

African Missionary, The. Cork.

Anthologia Hibernica. Dublin.

Ar Aghaidh. Galway.

Archivium Hibernicum. Maynooth.

Béaloideas. Dublin.

Bell, The. Dublin.

Calendar of State Papers, Ireland, James I, 1611–1614. London, 1877.

Claidheamh Soluis, An. Dublin.

Cornhill Magazine, The. London.

Dublin and London Magazine, The. Dublin.

Dublin Penny Journal, The. Dublin.

Dublin University Magazine. Dublin.

Eriú. Dublin.

The Ethnography of the Mullet, Inishkea Islands, and Portacloy, Co. Mayo. Proceedings R.I. Academy, 3rd ser., Vol. 3, 1893–96.

The Ethnography of Carna and Mweenish, in the Parish of Moyruss, Connemara. Proceedings R.I. Academy, 3rd ser., Vol. 6, 1900–02.

The Ethnography of Inishbofin and Inishshark, County Galway. Proceedings R.I. Academy, 3rd ser., Vol. 3, 1893–1896.

Father Matthew Record. Dublin.

Folk-Lore. London.

Folklore Record. London.

Handwörterbuch des deutschen Aberglaubens, V. Berlin, 1932–1933.

Idrottslekar. Questionnaire from Uppsala Landsmaalsarkivet, 1930.

Ireland's Own. Dublin.

Ireland Illustrated. Dublin.

Irish Catholic Directory. Dublin.

Irish Ecclesiastical Directory. Dublin.

Irish Fireside, The. Dublin.

Irish Independent. Dublin.

Irish Packet, The. Dublin.

Irisleabhar na Gaedhilge. Dublin.

Irländische Erzählungen, I–II. Breslau, 1826.

Journal of the Ardagh and Clonmacnoise Antiquarian Society. Longford.

Journal of the Kildare Archæological Society. Dublin.

Journal of the Kilkenny Archæological Society (J.R.S.A.I.).

Lóchrann, An. Cork.

Metrical Dindshenchas, The, III. ed. by Edward Gwynn. R.I. Academy: Todd Lecture Series, X, 1913.

Montgomeryshire Collections, The. Welshpool, 1951.

Parliamentary Gazeteer of Ireland. Dublin, 1846.

Pastoral Instructions for the Diocese of Kildare and Leighlin for the Lent of 1821. Carlow, 1821.

Rennes Dindshenchas, The. ed. by Whitley Stokes (*Revue Celtique* XVI, 1895). Paris.

Revue des Traditions Populaires. Paris, 1890.

Saint Patrick's. Dublin.

Salmagundi. Dublin.

Scottish Notes and Queries. Aberdeen, 1888–.

Shamrock, The. Dublin.

Spicilegium Ossoriense (Moran, Rev. P. F.). Dublin, 1874.

Statistical Account of Scotland, The. Edinburgh, 1791–1798.

Statuta Dioecesana in Dioecesi Ardacadensi observanda. Dublin, 1834.

Statuta Dioecesana per Provinciam Dublinensem observanda. Dublin, 1831.

Statuta Dioecesis Fernensis. Dublin, 1898.

Statuta Synodalia pro unitis dioecesibus Cassel et Imelac. Dublin, 1813.

Stoc, An. Galway.

Transactions of the Royal Irish Academy. Dublin.

Ulster Review, The. Belfast.

Whitefriars. Dublin.

INDEX

185

MORE MERCIER BESTSELLERS

LETTERS FROM THE GREAT BLASKET

Eibhlís Ní Shúilleabháin

This selection of *Letters from the Great Blasket*, for the most part written by Eibhlís Ní Shúilleabháin of the island to George Chambers in London, covers a period of over twenty years. Eibhlís married Seán Ó Criomhthain – a son of Tomás Ó Criomhthain, An tOileánach (The Islandman). On her marriage she lived in the same house as the Islandman and nursed him during the last years of his life which are described in the letters. Incidentally, the collection includes what must be an unique specimen of the Islandman's writing in English in the form of a letter expressing his goodwill towards Chambers.

Beginning in 1931 when the island was still a place where one might marry and raise a family (if only for certain exile in America) the letters end in 1951 with the author herself in exile on the mainland and 'the old folk of the island scattering to their graves'. By the time Eibhlís left the Blasket in July 1942 the island school had already closed and the three remaining pupils 'left to run wild with the rabbits'.

MÉINÍ
THE BLASKET NURSE

LESLIE MATSON

This is the life story of a remarkable woman, Méiní Dunlevy. Born in Massachusetts of Kerry parents, Méiní was reared in her grandparents' house in Dunquin. When she was nineteen, she eloped with an island widower to the Great Blasket, where she worked as a nurse and midwife for thirty-six years. Returning widowed to Dunquin, she died in 1967, aged 91.

Méiní's story, recorded by the author from her own accounts and those of her friends and relatives in Dunquin, is an evocation of a forceful, spicy personality and a compelling reconstruction of a way of life that has exercised an enduring fascination for readers. *Méiní, the Blasket Nurse* is a worthy successor to *An t-Oileánach* and *Twenty Years a-Growing*.

TOSS THE FEATHERS
IRISH SET DANCING

PAT MURPHY

Toss the Feathers provides a comprehensive approach to set dancing. It contains sixty-four complete set dances, including all those danced commonly in classes, summer schools and at feiseanna. These are laid out in conventional set terminology and can be easily followed by teachers, pupils and anyone who has an acquaintance with the art of set dancing. The book also contains the first concise history of the development of set dancing in Ireland from its eighteenth-century European origins.

IN MY FATHER'S TIME

EAMON KELLY

In My Father's Time invites us to a night of storytelling by Ireland's greatest and best loved seanchaí, Eamon Kelly. The fascinating stories reveal many aspects of Irish life and character. There are tales of country customs, matchmaking, courting, love, marriage and the dowry system, emigration, American wakes and returned emigrants. The stream of anecdotes never runs dry and the humour sparkles and illuminates the stories.

THINGS IRISH

ANTHONY BLUETT

Things Irish provides the reader with an entertaining and informative view of Ireland, seen through the practices, beliefs and everyday objects that seem to belong specifically to this country. Discarding the usual format of chapters on a variety of themes, the book uses short descriptive passages on anything from whisky to standing stones, from May Day to hurling, in order to create a distinctive image of Irish life. The reader is free to roam from topic to topic, from passage to passage, discovering a wealth of new and surprising facts and having a number of misguided beliefs put right.

THE GREAT IRISH FAMINE

EDITED BY CATHAL PÓIRTÉIR

This is the most wide-ranging series of essays ever published on the Great Irish Famine and will prove of lasting interest to the general reader. Leading historians, economist, geographers – from Ireland, Britain and the United States – have assembled the most up-to-date research from a wide spectrum of disciplines, including medicine, folklore and literature, to give the fullest account yet of the background and consequences of the Famine.